SPIRITUAL
STONES

MUHAMMAD BAYAZEED

SPIRITUAL STONES

STONES MAKE MOUNTAINS

IBN MISBAH BOOKS

Author	Muhammad Bayazeed
Title	Spiritual Stones
Subtitle	Stones Make Mountains
Publisher	Ibn Misbah Books
Cover Design	Muhammad Bayazeed
Illustrations	Muhammad Bayazeed

Dedication

For my parents and grandparents.

They have sacrificed their lives and dreams to see me build mine. I could never compensate them for all they have done. I hope that Allah Ta'ala accepts this work alongside all future works and services as a means of endless reward for them.

May Allah Ta'ala fill their lives and hereafters with happiness and blessings. May Allah Ta'ala reward them in full for every bit of sacrifice and effort they have ever made. May Allah Ta'ala gift them with the highest of ranks and greatest of honours in this world and the next. May Allah Ta'ala overlook their shortcomings and protect them from all forms of harm and evil. May Allah Ta'ala keep them forever under the shade of His special love and mercy.

Oh my Allah,

It is not in my ability to payback or reward such great people,

Such mighty tasks I leave with You.

Turn their every teardrop into an ocean of blessings,

Please them and with them be pleased too.

Aameen.

Oh my Allah,

In the gardens of Your love and mercy,
even the broken tree can bear fruit.

Bayazeed

Contents

Foreword

بسم الله الرحمن الرحيم، الحمد لله ربّ العالمين والصلاة والسلام على رسول الله صلّى الله عليه وسلّم وعلى آله وأصحابه ومن تبعهم بإحسان إلى يوم الدين.

"In the name of Allah, The Most Gracious, The Most Merciful. All praise is for Allah Ta'ala, The Master of all the worlds. Peace and salutations be upon The Messenger of Allah (Peace Be Upon Him), and upon his family and companions and all those who rightfully follow them until the last day."

Spirituality is an often-overlooked matter. In a world captured by materialism and worldly glamour, such things are frequently given the back seat. Ignored as it may be, spirituality has been deeply emphasised by the Shariah.

Focusing on the external is a naturally understood matter, alongside such focus though, it is of crucial importance to purify one's internal state. In fact, only after such inner purification can an individual truly appreciate the sweetness of faith and pleasure of worship. Highlighting and emphasising all such forms of purification, Prophet Muhammad (Peace Be Upon Him) teaches us in a Hadith:

الطهور شطر الإيمان (رواه مسلم)

Translation: "Purification is half of faith." (Muslim)

The essence of spirituality is to improve the inner being such that it reflects onto the external being. It is exactly with this focus, hoping to display the strong link between one's internal state and exterior being that the second Caliph, Umar (May Allah Be Pleased with Him) mentioned:

من قل حياؤه قل ورعه، ومن قل ورعه مات قلبه (مكارم الاخلاق)

Translation: "Whoever decreases in their modesty, decreases in their piety, and whoever decreases in their piety, their heart shall die." (Makarim al-Akhlaaq)

Through the grace and mercy of Almighty Allah Ta'ala, Mufti Muhammad Bayazeed has compiled a valuable collection of spiritual teachings. Authentically sourced from the Holy Qur'an and Hadith, and filled with potential to deeply help people from all walks of life, Spiritual Stones is filled with beautiful reminders and heart touching messages.

We ask Allah Ta'ala to accept this work and make it a means of great benefit for humanity at large. We ask Allah Ta'ala to accept Mufti Bayazeed and make this a means of endless elevation for him in this world and the next. We further ask Allah Ta'ala to make this book a means of continuous reward for Mufti Bayazeed and all his associates. Aameen.

Mufti Abdul-Samad Ahmed

Jamiatul-Ilm Wal-Huda

Blackburn, UK

19th Rajab 1443 / 20th February 2022

Introduction

To drastically transform every aspect of one's life and completely change in one night is no demand from Allah Ta'ala and neither His expectation. Spirituality and closeness with Allah Ta'ala is a journey; a rigorous journey, a lifelong journey.

The believer is not expected to attain perfection, rather to work towards perfection. In all one's life it is quite possible that one may never become perfect, and neither will that matter. What will matter in the courts of Allah Ta'ala is the efforts one made.

Allah Ta'ala seeks not results or achievements from us, in fact, it is our efforts and sacrifice that He seeks. The believer desires not to journey to an end, but to keep progressing and ultimately die upon this path.

Every moment and experience in one's spiritual journey is but a stepping stone towards ultimate success. It may not be in any person's might to make mountain loads of changes, but it is every individual's duty to do what is in their capacity, albeit a stone. One spiritual stone at a time, every believer can build a mountain of faith.

Muhammad Bayazeed

December 2021

Oh my Allah,

With a single step I begin this journey,
If a fall is destined, to the end carry me.

Bayazeed

Spiritual Stone 1

Allah Ta'ala is The Creator and The Master. Allah Ta'ala is The First and The Last. Allah Ta'ala was there when there was nothing, and Allah Ta'ala will remain when there will no longer be anything. Allah Ta'ala is the eternal being, the ever-living being, the being Who sees no end. For every other being, there was a time when they had no life, and again a time will come when their life will be taken away. Allah Ta'ala says in the Holy Qur'an:

كُلُّ نَفْسٍ ذَائِقَةُ الْمَوْتِ ﴿١٨٥ آل عمران﴾

Translation: *"Every soul shall taste death"* (Al-Imran/185)

Every man will taste death and every woman will taste death. The rich will taste death and the poor will taste death. The knowledgeable will taste death and the ignorant will taste death. The honoured will taste death and the fools will taste death. The angel of death will also taste death.

If this world were to remain for any soul in it,

The messenger of Allah's life would be infinite.

The beloved of Allah Ta'ala, the leader of mankind had to taste death, and what a sad day it was! The companions (May Allah Be Pleased with Them) were taken by shock. They couldn't believe what they were witnessing.

Their minds were shaken, and their hearts were shattered,

Their courage had crumbled, their bodies were battered.

It was a first for the books of history. Without doubt, history had never witnessed a day like this before, and without doubt, history will never witness a day like this again.

The trauma left the companions (May Allah Be Pleased with Them) in a state of absolute devastation. Even the likes of Umar (May Allah Be Pleased with Him), a man that dominantly stood firm against every evil, injustice and oppression, a man like this was left unstable.

Allah Ta'ala had chosen one man for that day, Allah Ta'ala had filled that man's heart with strength and light; that man was Abu Bakr (May Allah Be Pleased with Him).

After witnessing everything, Abu Bakr (May Allah Be Pleased with Him) stood in front of the companions and began to address them:

أيها الناس، من كان يعبد محمداً، فإن محمداً قد مات، ومن كان يعبد الله، فإن الله حي لا يموت

Translation: *"Oh people! Whoever worships Muhammad, let him know that Muhammad has indeed passed away, and whoever worships Allah, let him know that Allah is The-Eternal, he shall never pass away!"*

He further recited the verse of Allah Ta'ala:

وَمَا مُحَمَّدٌ إِلَّا رَسُولٌ قَدْ خَلَتْ مِنْ قَبْلِهِ الرُّسُلُ ۚ أَفَإِنْ مَاتَ أَوْ قُتِلَ انْقَلَبْتُمْ عَلَىٰ أَعْقَابِكُمْ ۚ وَمَنْ يَنْقَلِبْ عَلَىٰ عَقِبَيْهِ فَلَنْ يَضُرَّ اللَّهَ شَيْئًا ۗ وَسَيَجْزِي اللَّهُ الشَّاكِرِينَ ﴿١٤٤ آل عمران﴾

Translation: *"And Muhammad is no more than a messenger of Allah. There were many messengers before him that also passed away. If Muhammad is to pass away or be killed, does that mean you will turn back on your heels and return to your old ways? And whosoever turns back on his heels and goes back to his old ways, let him know that his choice will not harm Allah in the least. However, those who are grateful (those who remain firm upon truth and servitude to Allah), soon Allah will reward them"* (Al-Imran/144)

This verse of Allah Ta'ala brought the companions (May Allah Be Pleased with Them) back into their senses. The verse had been revealed before, but it was as though they had heard it for the first time.

Reflect servant of Allah, reflect! Reflect before your heart becomes so covered in dirt that your left with no ability to reflect. Reflect before permanent decisions are made, leaving no benefit for you to reflect. Reflect before you are left with no time to reflect. Reflect before there is no reason left to reflect.

How many moments and hours have been spent reflecting over things that have no guarantee, and how many moments and hours have been spent reflecting over that which we cannot escape?

How many days and weeks have been spent worrying for the doubtful and unknown, and how many days and weeks have been spent worrying about the definite and known?

How many years and lifetimes have passed preparing for that which is to end, and how many years have we given in preparation for that which is to last?

May Allah Ta'ala grant us life for as long as life is good for us. May Allah Ta'ala let our deaths be a gift for us and not a burden. May Allah Ta'ala let our deaths be a passionate meeting of lovers for us and not a sorrowful separation.

اللَّهُمَّ اجْعَلْ خَيْرَ عُمْرِي آخِرَهُ، وَخَيْرَ عَمَلِي خَوَاتِمَهُ، وَاجْعَلْ خَيْرَ أَيَّامِي يَوْمَ أَلْقَاكَ (مجمع الزوائد)

Translation: *"Oh Allah! Let the ending stages of my life be its best, let the best of my deeds be my last, and let the best of my days be the day that I meet You!"* (Majma'uz Zawaid)

آمين يا رب! آمين يا رب! آمين يا رب!

Accept our prayers, our Master! Accept our prayers, our Master! Accept our prayers! Accept our prayers, our Master!

Oh my Allah,

Death to every desire before You,
And what is life, but death?
Only without You.

Bayazeed

Spiritual Stone 2

Allah Ta'ala is The All-Powerful Being. He is The Originator of the heavens and the earth. For Him is kingship over all that exists within them, and for Him is kingship over all that exists beyond them. The power is His, the ownership is His, and the command is His. He takes no permission, and none can question Him. Allah Ta'ala says in the Holy Qur'an:

تَبَارَكَ الَّذِي بِيَدِهِ الْمُلْكُ وَهُوَ عَلَىٰ كُلِّ شَيْءٍ قَدِيرٌ ﴿١﴾ الَّذِي خَلَقَ الْمَوْتَ وَالْحَيَاةَ لِيَبْلُوَكُمْ أَيُّكُمْ أَحْسَنُ عَمَلًا ۚ
وَهُوَ الْعَزِيزُ الْغَفُورُ ﴿٢ الملك﴾

Translation: *"Blessed is Allah, in Whose hands lie complete authority and kingship, the being Who possesses all power and is capable of all things. The being that created both life and death to test you and see who amongst you is best in character and deed, and He is The-Almighty, The-Forgiving!"* (Al-Mulk/1-2)

Allah Ta'ala has created this world to test us, and to see who amongst us is best in his deed and character. He created life to test us, and He created death to test us. Life in this world, and death in this world may appear as two completely different things, but the purpose is one, the testing of mankind. At different times, different people will be tested through different things, but let no person assume that they are not being tested.

At times a person may be tested through blessings, at others through affliction. At times a person may be tested through power, at others through weakness. At times a person may be tested through wealth, at others through need. At times a person may be tested through fame, at others through loneliness. Whatever the case and whoever the person, every person shall be tested.

The world is for testing, and for testing it shall be,

Weak, strong, old, or young, it is the lord's decree.

At every moment Allah Ta'ala is watching to see what deeds we are presenting before Him and how we are reacting to the situations He puts before us. Every moment is an opportunity to present a good deed before Allah Ta'ala, and every moment is a chance to gain the pleasure of Allah Ta'ala.

Am I remembering Allah Ta'ala in my moment of happiness, am I allowing this moment of happiness to bring me closer to Allah Ta'ala? Am I reflecting during this moment of pain, am I allowing this moment of pain to save me from the punishment of the fire? Am I using these blessings of Allah Ta'ala for His sake, are these blessings taking me into paradise?

Question yourself dear friend, question yourself before the questioning begins. Correct yourself dear friend, correct yourself before the fire is the only thing left to correct you.

Let no happiness be wasted, and let no pain be wasted,

Let no blessing be wasted, and let no affliction be wasted,

Moments are to go, and deeds are to stay,

The sweet shall be tasted, and the bitter shall be tasted,

Goodness shall be tasted, and badness shall be tasted.

May Allah Ta'ala let our every moment and every ability be for His sake. May Allah Ta'ala let every situation that comes upon us be a means of gaining His closeness and happiness. May Allah Ta'ala make us from those who constantly remember Him and turn to Him. May

Allah Ta'ala allow us to be pleased with His every wish and may Allah Ta'ala be pleased with us.

رَبَّنَا تَقَبَّلْ مِنَّا إِنَّكَ أَنْتَ السَّمِيعُ الْعَلِيمُ ﴿١٢٧﴾ رَبَّنَا وَاجْعَلْنَا مُسْلِمَيْنِ لَكَ وَمِنْ ذُرِّيَّتِنَا أُمَّةً مُسْلِمَةً لَكَ وَأَرِنَا مَنَاسِكَنَا وَتُبْ عَلَيْنَا إِنَّكَ أَنْتَ التَّوَّابُ الرَّحِيمُ ﴿١٢٨ البقرة﴾

Translation: *"Oh our Master! Accept our deeds and what we present before You, verily You are The All-Hearing, The All-Knowing. Oh our Master! Make us such people that submit and surrender before You, make such people from our offspring that submit and surrender before You, teach us how to worship You and accept our repentance. Indeed, You are The Accepter of Repentance, The Most Merciful"* (Al-Baqarah/127-128)

آمين يا رب! آمين يا رب! آمين يا رب!

"Accept our prayers, our Master! Accept our prayers, our Master! Accept our prayers, our Master!

Oh my Allah,

Melt me away in Your love,
Make me water before You.

Hold me and throw me,
As You please, let me too.

Bayazeed

Allah Ta'ala is The All-Knowing, the being with perfect knowledge of all, knowledge beyond comprehension. Allah Ta'ala is The All-Wise, the being with perfect wisdom, unfathomable wisdom. Allah Ta'ala says in the Holy Qur'an:

الم ﴿١﴾ أَحَسِبَ النَّاسُ أَنْ يُتْرَكُوا أَنْ يَقُولُوا آمَنَّا وَهُمْ لَا يُفْتَنُونَ ﴿٢﴾ وَلَقَدْ فَتَنَّا الَّذِينَ مِنْ قَبْلِهِمْ فَلَيَعْلَمَنَّ اللَّهُ الَّذِينَ صَدَقُوا وَلَيَعْلَمَنَّ الْكَاذِبِينَ ﴿٣ العنكبوت﴾

Translation: *"Alif Lam Mim. Did people think that they were just going to say that they believe and then be left alone without being put through affliction and trial? Certainly, we tested all those before them with trial and affliction. Like this, through affliction and trial, Allah distinguished between those who are true to their word and those who are liars"* (Al-Ankabut/1-3)

Oh Believers! What were you thinking? Were you thinking it was going to be easy? Were you thinking you were going to enter paradise just like that? Did you really think that all you had to do was to utter a few words and then you were going to be rewarded forever with happiness and pleasure? The Prophet of Allah (Peace Be Upon Him) says in a Hadith:

حُفَّتِ الْجَنَّةُ بِالْمَكَارِهِ وَحُفَّتِ النَّارُ بِالشَّهَوَاتِ (رواه مسلم)

Translation: *"Paradise is surrounded by adversity and affliction; the fire of hell is surrounded by desires and lust"* (Muslim)

Adversity and affliction in this world are the believer's doorway to paradise. No person desires affliction, but every believer has a longing for paradise.

Do not be saddened by the hardship Oh Believer, be pleased with what waits behind it. This is the decision of Allah Ta'ala, a decision made with His perfect knowledge and wisdom, knowledge and wisdom far beyond ours. This is his way, and none can change it, not even you and your sadness. In another Hadith the Prophet of Allah (Peace Be Upon Him) is reported to have said:

إن عِظَم الجزاء من عِظَم البلاء، وإن الله إذا أحب قوماً ابتلاهم، فمن رضي فله الرضا، ومن سخط فله السخط
(رواه الترمذي وابن ماجه)

Translation: *"The greatest of rewards are through the greatest of trials, and when Allah Ta'ala loves a people, He puts them through trial and affliction. The one who is content and happily accepts the decision of Allah Ta'ala, for him is happiness and contentment. The one who is displeased and saddened by this decision of Allah Ta'ala, for him is sadness and displeasure"* (Tirmidhi and Ibn Majah)

The greatest of rewards are gained through the greatest of trials. Oh Believer, do not be disheartened by the overwhelming nature of the difficulty, be overjoyed by the overwhelming reward that awaits you.

The more Allah Ta'ala loves a person, the more he is tested. Oh Believer, do not be broken by the hardship, let the love of Allah Ta'ala hold you together.

Let the days do as they please,

Be content with the decision sent your way.

Fear not the nights and what is to come,

Nothing of this world is here to stay.

May Allah Ta'ala grant us strength and courage. May Allah Ta'ala be our hope and our shelter. May Allah Ta'ala be our friend and our protector.

رَبَّنَا لَا تُؤَاخِذْنَا إِنْ نَسِينَا أَوْ أَخْطَأْنَا ۚ رَبَّنَا وَلَا تَحْمِلْ عَلَيْنَا إِصْرًا كَمَا حَمَلْتَهُ عَلَى الَّذِينَ مِنْ قَبْلِنَا ۚ رَبَّنَا وَلَا تُحَمِّلْنَا مَا لَا طَاقَةَ لَنَا بِهِ ۖ وَاعْفُ عَنَّا وَاغْفِرْ لَنَا وَارْحَمْنَا ۚ أَنْتَ مَوْلَانَا فَانْصُرْنَا عَلَى الْقَوْمِ الْكَافِرِينَ ﴿٢٨٦ البقرة﴾

Translation: *"Oh our Lord! Do not take us to task or punish us for being forgetful or making mistakes. Oh our Lord! Do not burden us like those before us were burdened. Oh our Lord! Do not test us with more than we can bear! Pardon us, forgive us, and have mercy upon us. You are our protector and guardian, help us against those who disbelieve"* (Al-Baqarah/286)

آمين يا رب! آمين يا رب! آمين يا رب!

"Accept our prayers, our Master! Accept our prayers, our Master! Accept our prayers, our Master!

Oh my Allah,

Fascinating not is my love for You,
You are The King of All, Eternal Beauty.

I am but a weak, sinful slave.
Oh how You still love me!

Bayazeed

Allah Ta'ala is The All-Seeing, the being Who sees even the most hidden of things with full clarity. Allah Ta'ala is The All-Hearing, the being who attentively hears even the deepest whispers of the heart. Allah Ta'ala says in the Holy Qur'an:

$$\text{أَوَلَا يَعْلَمُونَ أَنَّ اللَّهَ يَعْلَمُ مَا يُسِرُّونَ وَمَا يُعْلِنُونَ ﴿٧٧ البقرة﴾}$$

Translation: "*Do they not know that Allah Ta'ala is fully aware of all that they show and all that they hide?*" (Al-Baqarah/77)

Allah Ta'ala is fully aware of all things, nothing can be kept away from Him. It is possible for man to be deceived, but Allah Ta'ala can never be deceived. It is possible for something to slip the sight and hearing of man, but nothing can slip past the sight and hearing of Allah Ta'ala. In another verse Allah Ta'ala says:

$$\text{قُلْ إِنْ تُخْفُوا مَا فِي صُدُورِكُمْ أَوْ تُبْدُوهُ يَعْلَمْهُ اللَّهُ ۗ وَيَعْلَمُ مَا فِي السَّمَاوَاتِ وَمَا فِي الْأَرْضِ ۚ وَاللَّهُ عَلَى كُلِّ شَيْءٍ قَدِيرٌ}$$
$$\text{﴿٢٩ آل عمران﴾}$$

Translation: "*Say to them, whether you conceal what is in your hearts or bring it into the open, Allah knows it, for He knows all that is in the heavens and all that is on earth; and Allah has the power to do all things*" (Al-Imran/29)

Oh Mankind! Excuses may have saved you from the people, but what excuse will save you from Allah Ta'ala? Oh Mankind! You may get away from the clutches of man, but what will release you from the hold of Allah Ta'ala?

Oh Mankind! You may be walking freely, feeling you have escaped, but do you not know that Allah Ta'ala is capable of all things? Do you not know that Allah Ta'ala can bring before you all that you ever thought you had hidden? It is narrated from Abu Hurairah (May Allah Be Pleased with Him) that the Prophet (Peace Be Upon Him) said:

إن أول الناس يُقضى يوم القيامة عليه رجُل اسْتُشْهِدَ، فأُتِي به، فعرَّفه نِعمته، فعرَفَها، قال: فما عَمِلت فيها؟ قال: قَاتَلْتُ فيك حتى اسْتُشْهِدْتُ. قال: كَذَبْتَ، ولكنك قَاتَلْتَ لأن يقال: جَرِيءٌ! فقد قيل، ثم أُمِرَ به فَسُحِب على وجهه حتى أُلقِي في النار. ورجل تعلم العلم وعلمه، وقرأ القرآن، فأُتِي به فعرَّفه نِعَمه فعرَفَها. قال: فما عملت فيها؟ قال: تعلمت العلم وعلمته، وقرأت فيك القرآن، قال: كَذَبْتَ، ولكنك تعلمت ليقال: عالِمٌ! وقرأت القرآن ليقال: هو قارئٌ؛ فقد قيل، ثم أُمِرَ به فَسُحِب على وجهه حتى أُلقِي في النار. ورجل وَسَّعَ الله عليه، وأعطاه من أصناف المال، فأُتِي به فعرَّفه نِعَمه، فعرَفَها. قال: فما عملت فيها؟ قال: ما تركت من سبيل تُحِبُّ أن يُنْفَقَ فيها إلا أنفقت فيها لك. قال: كَذَبْتَ، ولكنك فعلت ليقال: جوادٌ! فقد قيل، ثم أُمِرَ به فَسُحِب على وجهه حتى أُلقِي في النار (رواه مسلم)

Translation: *"Verily, from the first of people to be judged on the Day of Resurrection will be a man who had died as a martyr. He will be brought forward. Allah will remind him of the favours He had bestowed upon him and the man will acknowledge them. Then He will ask him: 'What did you do to express gratitude for it?' The man will reply: 'I fought for Your cause till I was martyred.' Allah will say: `You have lied. You fought so that people might call you courageous; and they have done so.' Command will then be issued about him and he will be dragged on his face and thrown into Hell.*

Next a man who had acquired knowledge, imparted knowledge and read the Qur'an will be brought forward, Allah will remind him of the favours He had bestowed upon him and the man will acknowledge them. Then He will ask him: 'What did you do to express gratitude for it?' The man will reply: 'I acquired knowledge I taught it, and I read the Qur'an for Your sake.' Allah will say to him: `You have lied. You acquired knowledge so that people might call you a learned man, and you read the Qur'an so that they might call you a reciter, and they have done so.' Command will then be issued about him, and he will be dragged on his face and thrown into Hell.

Next a man whom Allah had made affluent and to whom Allah had given plenty of wealth, will be brought forward, Allah will remind him of the favours He had bestowed upon him and the man will acknowledge them. He will ask him: `What did you do to express gratitude for it?' The man will reply: 'I did not neglect any of the ways You liked wealth to be spent freely for Your sake'. Allah will say to him: `You have lied. You did it so that people might call you generous, and they have done so.' Command will then be issued about him and he will be dragged on his face and thrown into Hell." (Muslim)

Dear servant of Allah Ta'ala, what better royal garment can the body be dressed in than the priceless blood of a martyr? Dear servant of Allah Ta'ala, what can more beautifully adorn the tongue than sacred knowledge and the word of Allah Ta'ala? Dear servant of Allah Ta'ala, what can better raise the value of wealth than the spending of it in the path of Allah Ta'ala?

Gold or simply gold-plated,

The Creator knows best what He created.

May Allah Ta'ala grant us the ability to remain in constant awareness of Him. May Allah Ta'ala grant us true sincerity. May Allah Ta'ala save us from deceiving ourselves. May Allah Ta'ala save us from hypocrisy and grant us the ability to truly gain his pleasure. May Allah Ta'ala allow us to put His pleasure before all other pleasures, even our own.

آمین یا رب! آمین یا رب! آمین یا رب!

"Accept our prayers, our Master! Accept our prayers, our Master! Accept our prayers, our Master!

Oh my Allah,

How You travel through my veins!
How You touch me like the wind!

How the world sees You far!
How I feel You within!

Bayazeed

All praise is for Allah Ta'ala, The Comforter; that being Who comforts the believer even in a state of utter distress. All praise is for Allah Ta'ala, The Listener; that being Who listens to the believer when there is none to hear him. All praise is for Allah Ta'ala, The Companion; that being Who remains in companionship with the believer, even when he has no other companion. The Prophet (Peace Be Upon Him) is narrated to have said:

المرء على دين خليله فلينظر أحدكم من يخالل (رواه أحمد)

Translation: *"A person is on the way of his friend, so each of you should be very cautious about who you make your friend"* (Ahmad)

Oh Servants of Allah! Be careful who you befriend, the Prophet of Allah (Peace Be Upon Him) has spoken. The Prophet of Allah (Peace Be Upon Him) was under the direct guidance of Allah Ta'ala.

This man (Peace Be Upon Him) gave up his every pleasure, so we could be rewarded with endless pleasure. Oh Servants of Allah! How can we disregard the advices of such a man, a man (Peace Be Upon Him) whose every thought revolved around me and you?

Rivers flowed from the Prophet's eyes in worry for you,

A concern for countless this man was put through,

Comfort left his soul seeking guidance for you,

Restless at every moment, if only you knew.

Allah Ta'ala says in the Holy Qur'an:

الْأَخِلَّاءُ يَوْمَئِذٍ بَعْضُهُمْ لِبَعْضٍ عَدُوٌّ إِلَّا الْمُتَّقِينَ ﴿٦٧ الزخرف﴾

Translation: *"On that day, close friends will be enemies to one another, except for the righteous"* (Az-Zukhruf/67)

What is the friendship of this world? Friends will be enemies on that day! The only friendship to remain is the friendship of the righteous. The only friendship to remain is that friendship which brings a person closer to Allah Ta'ala and his beloved Messenger (Peace Be Upon Him).

عَنْ عَمْرِو بْنِ عَبَسَة عَنِ النَّبِيِّ صَلَّى اللهُ عَلَيْهِ وَسَلَّمَ قَالَ قَالَ اللهُ تَعَالَى حَقَّتْ مَحَبَّتِي لِلَّذِينَ يَتَصَادَقُونَ مِنْ أَجْلِي وَحَقَّتْ مَحَبَّتِي لِلَّذِينَ يَتَنَاصَرُونَ مِنْ أَجْلِي (المعجم الصغير للطبراني)

Translation: *Amr ibn 'Abasah narrates from The Prophet (Peace Be Upon Him), "Allah Almighty has said: My love is a right upon those who befriend each other for my sake. My love is a right upon those who defend and help one another for my sake"* (Al-Mu'jam as-Saghir)

What greater blessing can there be than the love of Allah Ta'ala! What can a believer desire more than the love of Allah Ta'ala! What can be more comforting and pleasurable than the love of Allah Ta'ala!

Friendship for the sake of Allah Ta'ala, is a doorway to the divine love of Allah Ta'ala. Friendship for anything other than Allah Ta'ala is a doorway to disaster.

Friendship for the sake of Allah Ta'ala is true friendship. Friendship for anything other than Allah Ta'ala, is in fact enmity. So let each person choose his friends wisely.

The friends of comfort and ease are many,

Friends in calamity are only a few,

The changing of times will leave you friendless,

Do not be deceived by all who befriend you.

Each person claims of his sincerity,

Not all are true to what they say,

A man of his word is only that friend,

A noble friend, upon god's way.

May Allah Ta'ala open our hearts to accept His teachings and the teachings of His beloved Messenger (Peace Be Upon Him). May Allah Ta'ala bless us all with the gift of righteous friends and friendship for His sake. May Allah Ta'ala allow us all to be true and righteous friends for one another. May Allah Ta'ala bless us all with His love and may Allah Ta'ala unite us in paradise with all the prophets, martyrs, and pious predecessors.

آمين يا رب! آمين يا رب! آمين يا رب!

"Accept our prayers, our Master! Accept our prayers, our Master! Accept our prayers, our Master!

Oh my Allah,

To hear Your name echo through the heavens,
To see You from distance, standing before me.

What does the world know of pleasure?
You are the only pleasure to be!

Bayazeed

All praise is for Allah Ta'ala, The Acceptor. Allah Ta'ala is the being that accepts efforts, even the smallest of efforts. Allah Ta'ala is the being that accepts deeds, even deeds unworthy to be presented in His majestic court. Allah Ta'ala is the being that accepts repentance, even repentance followed by sin. Allah Ta'ala says in the Holy Qur'an:

أَمَّنْ يُجِيبُ الْمُضْطَرَّ إِذَا دَعَاهُ وَيَكْشِفُ السُّوءَ وَيَجْعَلُكُمْ خُلَفَاءَ الْأَرْضِ ۗ أَإِلَهٌ مَعَ اللَّهِ ۚ قَلِيلًا مَا تَذَكَّرُونَ ٦٢
النمل ۞

Translation: *"Who is it that responds to the distressed person when he calls out to him? Who is it that relieves the suffering? Who is it that makes you successors on the earth? Could there be any divine power or god besides Allah? How little they reflect and how unmindful they are!"*. (An-Naml/62)

How often man calls out seeking help from other than Allah Ta'ala, and how often he is left disappointed with no response! How often man wishes for someone or something other than Allah Ta'ala to relieve him, and how often he is left alone to suffer! How often man wishes ease from creation, and how often he is left in hardship!

Does man not know that it is only Allah Ta'ala that can respond whenever He is called? Does man not know that it is only Allah Ta'ala that can remove a difficulty? Does man not know that it is Allah Ta'ala that grants ease?

It is Allah Ta'ala, and only Allah Ta'ala that responds whenever He is called. It is Allah Ta'ala, and only Allah Ta'ala that removes difficulty. It is Allah Ta'ala, and only Allah Ta'ala that grants ease. He is alone, He has no partner, and there is none like Him.

Abu Dharr (May Allah Be Pleased with Him) narrates from the Prophet (Peace Be Upon Him) that Allah Ta'ala says:

يا عبادي كلكم ضال إلا من هديته، فاستهدوني أهدكم، يا عبادي كلكم جائع إلا من أطعمته، فاستطعموني
أطعمكم، يا عبادي كلكم عار إلا من كسوته، فاستكسوني أكسكم، يا عبادي إنكم تخطئون بالليل والنهار، وأنا
أغفر الذنوب جميعا فاستغفروني أغفر لكم... يا عبادي لو أن أولكم وآخركم وإنسكم وجنكم قاموا في صعيد
واحد فسألوني، فأعطيت كل واحد مسألته ما نقص ذلك مما عندي إلا كما ينقص المخيط إذا أدخل البحر (رواه
مسلم)

Translation: "*Oh My servants! All of you are misguided except the one who I guide, so seek My guidance, I will guide you. Oh My servants! All of you are hungry except the one who I feed, so ask Me for food, I will feed you. Oh My servants! All of you are naked except the one who I clothe, so ask Me for clothes, I will clothe you. Oh My servants! You sin all through the night and all through the day, I am the one Who grants forgiveness, so seek forgiveness from Me, I shall forgive you... Oh My servants! If the first of you, the last of you, the human of you, and the jinn of you, were to all gather on one plain asking me and seeking from me and I was to grant each, all that he requested, that would not decrease anything from my treasures, except like the decreasing of water by a needle when it is placed in the sea*" (Muslim)

So often people are unable to listen, whereas Allah Ta'ala eagerly waits to listen at every moment. Why not speak to Allah Ta'ala.

So often people are incapable of understanding, whereas Allah Ta'ala fully understands every situation. Why not explain to Allah Ta'ala?

So often people dislike being asked, whereas Allah Ta'ala loves to be asked. Why not ask Allah Ta'ala?

So often people have nothing to give, whereas Allah Ta'ala has endless treasures. Why not take from Allah Ta'ala?

So often people are powerless to help even if they wished to do so, whereas Allah Ta'ala has complete power. Why not seek the help of Allah Ta'ala?

So often people are unaware how to assist, whereas Allah Ta'ala has complete knowledge. Why not seek the guidance of Allah Ta'ala?

Far away the world runs, close You stay and O how keen!

When nothing can be seen my Allah, it is only You that can be seen!

All turns, near You stay, attentively You hear,

With me You are my Allah, what have I to fear?

You love to be asked, and how You love to be beseeched,

With You are the answers, in You I have believed!

May Allah Ta'ala be enough for us. May Allah Ta'ala grant us the ability to constantly turn to Him. May Allah Ta'ala let us take from His treasures. May Allah Ta'ala always hear our prayers and take care of all our needs. May our relationship with Allah Ta'ala be everlasting and intimate. May Allah Ta'ala please us all, and may He bless us with His pleasure.

آمين يا رب! آمين يا رب! آمين يا رب!

"Accept our prayers, our Master! Accept our prayers, our Master! Accept our prayers, our Master!

Oh my Allah,

Let the world sleep away,
Let darkness be our cover.

Let silence be our speech,
Let us be the each in other.

Bayazeed

Allah Ta'ala is The-Giver. The being that gives as He wishes. Allah Ta'ala gives whatever He likes to whoever He likes. Allah Ta'ala gives however He likes and whenever He likes. Allah Ta'ala is The-Taker. The being that takes as He wishes. Allah Ta'ala takes whatever He wants from whoever He wants. Allah Ta'ala takes however He wants and whenever He wants. What He gives none can take, and what He takes none can give. Allah Ta'ala says in the Holy Qur'an:

قُلِ اللَّهُمَّ مَالِكَ الْمُلْكِ تُؤْتِي الْمُلْكَ مَنْ تَشَاءُ وَتَنْزِعُ الْمُلْكَ مِمَّنْ تَشَاءُ وَتُعِزُّ مَنْ تَشَاءُ وَتُذِلُّ مَنْ تَشَاءُ بِيَدِكَ الْخَيْرُ إِنَّكَ عَلَى كُلِّ شَيْءٍ قَدِيرٌ ﴿٢٦ آل عمران﴾

Translation: *"Say! Oh Allah, You are The King of all kings, The Master over every Authority! You give power and authority to whoever You wish, and You take away power and authority from whoever You wish. You give honour to whoever You wish, and You take away honour from whoever You wish. All goodness is in Your hands; it is You that holds power over all things." (Al-Imran/26)*

Oh Mankind! If it is power you seek, then know very well that power lies in the hands of Allah Ta'ala. If entire creation wishes to remove power from a person, but Allah Ta'ala wishes to give him power, none can remove his power. Allah Ta'ala gives power to whoever He likes, and Allah Ta'ala takes away power from whoever He likes.

Oh Mankind! If it is wealth you seek, then know very well that wealth lies in the hands of Allah Ta'ala. If entire creation wishes to take away the wealth of a person, but Allah Ta'ala wishes to give him wealth, none can take away his wealth. Allah Ta'ala gives wealth to whoever He likes, and Allah Ta'ala takes away wealth from whoever He likes.

Oh Mankind! If it is honour you seek, then know very well that honour lies in the hands of Allah Ta'ala. If entire creation wishes to remove a person's honour, but Allah Ta'ala wishes to honour him, none can remove his honour. Allah Ta'ala gives honour to whoever He likes, and Allah Ta'ala takes away honour from whoever He likes.

Oh Mankind! If it is peace you seek, then know very well that peace lies in the hands of Allah Ta'ala. If entire creation wishes to remove a person's peace, but Allah Ta'ala wishes peace for him, none can remove his peace. Allah Ta'ala gives peace to whoever He likes, and Allah Ta'ala takes away peace from whoever He likes.

Oh Mankind! If it is security you seek, then know very well that security lies in the hands of Allah Ta'ala. If the entire creation wishes to remove a person's security, but Allah Ta'ala wishes security for him, none can remove his security. Allah Ta'ala gives security to whoever He likes, and Allah Ta'ala takes away security from whoever He likes.

Oh Mankind! If it is pleasure you seek, then know very well that pleasure lies in the hands of Allah Ta'ala. If the entire creation wishes to remove a person's pleasures, but Allah Ta'ala wishes pleasure for him, none can remove his pleasure. Allah Ta'ala gives pleasure to whoever He likes, and Allah Ta'ala takes away pleasure from whoever He likes.

Dear believer, power is for Allah Ta'ala and none but Him, so seek power from Him and only Him. The one who seeks power from other than Allah Ta'ala will be left with no power.

Dear believer, wealth is for Allah Ta'ala and none but Him, so seek wealth from Him and only Him. The one who seeks wealth from other than Allah Ta'ala will be left with no wealth.

Dear believer, honour is for Allah Ta'ala and none but Him, so seek honour from Him and only Him. The one who seeks honour from other than Allah Ta'ala will be left with no honour.

Dear believer, security is for Allah Ta'ala and none but Him, so seek security from Him and only Him. The one who seeks security from other than Allah Ta'ala will be left with no security.

Dear believer, peace is for Allah Ta'ala and none but Him, so seek peace from Him and only Him. The one who seeks peace from other than Allah Ta'ala will be left with no peace.

Dear believer, happiness is from Allah Ta'ala and none but Him, so seek happiness from Him and only Him. The one who seeks happiness from other than Allah Ta'ala will be left with no happiness.

You are my lord, my master and my creator,

For as long as I live to that I shall testify.

You are far beyond the words of those who are called besides You,

You are far noble, more great, most high.

The creation is Yours, the blessings are Yours, and the command is Yours,

In You we hope, You we worship, You we glorify.

رَبَّنَا لَا تُزِغْ قُلُوبَنَا بَعْدَ إِذْ هَدَيْتَنَا وَهَبْ لَنَا مِنْ لَدُنْكَ رَحْمَةً ۚ إِنَّكَ أَنْتَ الْوَهَّابُ ﴿٨ آل عمران﴾

Translation: *"Our Lord! Do not let our hearts turn away after You have guided us, and grant us Your mercy, You are The True Giver of all bounties."*
(Al-Imran/8)

آمين يا رب! آمين يا رب! آمين يا رب!

"Accept our prayers, our Master! Accept our prayers, our Master! Accept our prayers, our Master!

Oh my Allah,

You are the smiles in my joy,
You are the pleasure in my play.

You are the wish in my heart,
Reason for my stay.

Bayazeed

Praise be to Allah Ta'ala, The-Guide. Allah Ta'ala guides to the straight path whosoever He wishes. Whoever Allah Ta'ala guides, none can mislead. Whoever Allah Ta'ala leaves to go astray, none can guide.

The believer is constantly under the guidance of Allah Ta'ala. Allah Ta'ala guides through the Qur'an, through His messengers, through righteous servants, through creation all around, and even through direct inspiration.

How fortunate is the guided one! Guidance shall reach him even if it lies a million miles away. How unfortunate is the misguided one! Guidance will not reach him, even if it sits right before his very eyes. Allah Ta'ala guides mankind in the Holy Qur'an:

وَالْعَصْرِ ﴿١﴾ إِنَّ الْإِنْسَانَ لَفِي خُسْرٍ ﴿٢﴾ إِلَّا الَّذِينَ آمَنُوا وَعَمِلُوا الصَّالِحَاتِ وَتَوَاصَوْا بِالْحَقِّ وَتَوَاصَوْا بِالصَّبْرِ ﴿٣ العصر﴾

Translation: *"By the oath of time! Indeed, humanity is in a state of loss. Except for those who have faith, those who do good, those who encourage towards truth, and those who encourage patience and perseverance."* (Al-Asr/1-3)

Oh Man! What lets you play and what lets you laugh? Oh Man! What lets you sit idle and what lets you be thoughtless? Oh Man! Have you not heard the message of your creator?

How would it feel to know that all your wealth was slipping away from your fingertips piece by piece? How would it feel to know that all your loved ones were being separated from you one person at a time? How would it feel to know all the blood in your body was being drained away drop by drop?

Oh Man! Why are you able to sit thoughtless in play? Do you not know that the passing of every moment is separating you from your wealth? Do you not know that every passing second is breaking you away from your loved ones? Do you not know that your life is decreasing with every breath? The Prophet of Allah (Peace Be Upon Him) advises in a Hadith:

عَنْ أَبِي هُرَيْرَةَ رضي الله عنه أَنَّ رسولَ اللهِ صلَّى اللهُ عليه وسلَّم قال: بَادِرُوا بالأعْمَالِ سَبْعًا هل تنتظرون إلَّا فقْرًا مُنْسِيًا، أو غِنًى مُطْغِيًا، أو مرضًا مُفْسِدًا، أو هَرَمًا مُفْنِدًا، أو موتًا مُجْهِزًا، أو الدَّجَّالَ فشَرُّ غائِبٍ يُنْتظر، أو السَّاعَةَ فالسَّاعَةُ أَدْهَى وأَمَرُّ (رواه التِّرمذيُّ)

Translation: *"Hasten to do good before you are caught up by one of seven afflictions awaiting you! What are you waiting for? Are you waiting for such poverty that makes you forgetful of everything else? Are you waiting for such wealth and prosperity that leads you to corruption? Are you waiting to be overwhelmed by such a sickness that disables you? Are you waiting for such age that leaves you unstable? Are you waiting to be taken by a sudden death? Are you waiting for the Dajjal, the worst of all to be awaited? Or are you waiting for the final hour, which will be terrible and awfully bitter?"* (Tirmidhi)

Dear believer, you have been blessed with the ability to do good today, maybe you will be deprived of the ability tomorrow. Be quick to do good, be quick!

Dear believer, your book is still open for deeds to be written, you know not when it will close. Fill your book of deeds believer, fill your book of deeds!

Your Master waits for you dear believer! Dear believer, what are you waiting for?

Oh Allah! Let us spend our every moment in Your pleasure and save us from Your disobedience. Oh Allah! Give us the ability to do good before we are deprived of goodness. Oh Allah! Allow us to recognise You and Your blessings before we are brought before You for questioning. Oh Allah! Keep us firm upon guidance and save us from going astray.

رَبَّنَا ظَلَمْنَا أَنْفُسَنَا وَإِنْ لَمْ تَغْفِرْ لَنَا وَتَرْحَمْنَا لَنَكُونَنَّ مِنَ الْخَاسِرِينَ ﴿٢٣ الأعراف﴾

Translation: *"Oh our Master! We have oppressed ourselves. If You will not forgive us and have mercy upon us, we will definitely be from the losers"* (Al-A'araaf/23)

رَبَّنَا فَاغْفِرْ لَنَا ذُنُوبَنَا وَكَفِّرْ عَنَّا سَيِّئَاتِنَا وَتَوَفَّنَا مَعَ الْأَبْرَارِ ﴿١٩٣ آل عمران﴾

Translation: *"Oh our Master! Forgive us for our sins, wipe away our shortcomings, and let us die amongst the righteous."* (Al-Imran/193)

آمين يا رب! آمين يا رب! آمين يا رب!

"Accept our prayers, our Master! Accept our prayers, our Master! Accept our prayers, our Master!"

Oh my Allah,

Let us sleep away together,
Let me awaken in Your presence.

Let my every want be You,
Be my very essence.

Bayazeed

Praise be to You Allah, endless praise. Praise is for You as we praise You, praise is for You before we praise You, and praise is for You after we praise You. Praise be to You for letting us praise You, and praise be to You for letting us know your blessing in letting us praise You. With every praise, there is need for more praise. Our praising You is never enough, but we look to Your mercy Allah, accept our praise.

Compassion is Your name, Mercy too and Grace,

Love, love and love, for You is endless praise.

Allah Ta'ala says in the Holy Qur'an:

يَاأَيُّهَا الَّذِينَ آمَنُوا اتَّقُوا اللَّهَ حَقَّ تُقَاتِهِ وَلَا تَمُوتُنَّ إِلَّا وَأَنْتُمْ مُسْلِمُونَ ﴿١٠٢ آل عمران﴾

Translation: *"O Believers! Remain conscious of Allah in the way He deserves, and do not die except in a condition where you have fully surrendered yourself to him." (Al-Imran/102)*

Oh Allah I see You everywhere, and everything there is, You see,

I see You in the sky, in the stars, in the moon, even within me.

Your closeness is certain, I accept, yet my deeds show denial,

You are every moment, the moment without You is trial.

Heedless I am to Your attention and stay,

Human I am, what more can I say?

I forget You as You remember me,

Oh Lord, what can be said of my destiny?

Forgive me my Master,

Forgive all I have forgotten and all I will forget.

Wipe it all away dear lord,

My heart is in regret.

May Allah Ta'ala purify our hearts and forgive us for our weakness. May Allah Ta'ala wipe away our shortcomings and give us strength. May Allah Ta'ala remember us in every moment with His love, blessings and mercy. May our every moment be spent in His awareness and attention.

اللَّهُمَّ آتِ نَفْسِي تَقْوَاهَا، وَزَكِّهَا أَنْتَ خَيْرُ مَنْ زَكَّاهَا، أَنْتَ وَلِيُّهَا وَمَوْلَاهَا (رواه مسلم)

Translation: *"Oh Allah! Grant me the sense of piety, Your constant awareness, and purify my soul, for You are the best to purify it, You are its guardian and well-wisher"* (Muslim)

آمين يا رب! آمين يا رب! آمين يا رب!

"Accept our prayers, our Master! Accept our prayers, our Master! Accept our prayers, our Master!

Oh my Allah,

The oceans are for You,
How You love one tear drop from me.

Drops that put away the fire,
Dear eyes, such drops, let free.

Bayazeed

Oh Allah, You are The Protector, You give protection to all those who seek protection! Oh Allah, You are The Comforter, You comfort all those in discomfort! Oh Allah, You are The Helper, You help all those who are helpless!

Oh Allah, You are The Pillar and The Foundation, you provide support and rest to all those who have no support or rest! Oh Allah, You are The Creator of Means, You provide means for those who have no means! Oh Allah, You are The Ultimate Treasure, You shower Your treasures upon those in need! Oh Allah, You remind us in Your Holy Qur'an:

وَمَنْ يَتَّقِ اللَّهَ يَجْعَلْ لَهُ مَخْرَجًا ﴿٢﴾ وَيَرْزُقْهُ مِنْ حَيْثُ لَا يَحْتَسِبُ ۚ وَمَنْ يَتَوَكَّلْ عَلَى اللَّهِ فَهُوَ حَسْبُهُ ۚ ﴿٣ الطلاق﴾

Translation: *"And whosoever remains mindful of Allah Ta'ala, Allah Ta'ala will make a way out for him in every situation, Allah Ta'ala will provide for him in ways he could never expect. And whosoever trusts in Allah Ta'ala, Allah Ta'ala will be enough for them." (At-Talaq/2-3)*

Oh Allah, You are the greatest source of hope! Oh Allah, You are the saviour of those in ruin! Oh Allah, the brightness of the day bows before You! Oh Allah, the darkness of the night bows before You!

Oh Allah, the sun bows before You! Oh Allah, the moon bows before You! Oh Allah, the trees bow before You! Oh Allah, the rivers bow before You! Oh Allah, the mountains bow before You! Oh Allah, the skies bow before You.

Oh Allah, there is no power but You! Oh Allah, there is no hope but You! Oh Allah, there is no strength but You! Oh Allah, there is no help but You! Oh Allah, there is no need but You!

Oh Allah, we have no want but You! Oh Allah, we turn to You, and nobody but You! Oh Allah, we submit to You, and nobody but You! Oh Allah, we seek help from You, and nobody but You! Oh Allah, be for us, and let us be for You!

وَمَا تَوْفِيقِي إِلَّا بِاللهِ عَلَيْهِ تَوَكَّلْتُ وَإِلَيْهِ أُنِيبُ ﴿٨٨ هود﴾

Translation: *"And my success in any matter lies solely upon the help of Allah Ta'ala, in Him I place my trust and to Him I turn"* (Hud/88)

رَبَّنَا عَلَيْكَ تَوَكَّلْنَا وَإِلَيْكَ أَنَبْنَا وَإِلَيْكَ الْمَصِيرُ ﴿٤﴾ رَبَّنَا لَا تَجْعَلْنَا فِتْنَةً لِلَّذِينَ كَفَرُوا وَاغْفِرْ لَنَا رَبَّنَا إِنَّكَ أَنْتَ الْعَزِيزُ الْحَكِيمُ ﴿٥ الممتحنة﴾

Translation: *"Oh our Master, we have placed our trusts in You, we have turned to You, and to You is our return. Oh our Master, do not subject us to the persecution of those who are bent upon denying the truth, and Oh our lord, forgive our sins, indeed You are The-Almighty, The All-Wise."* (Al-Mumtahinah/4-5)

آمين يا رب! آمين يا رب! آمين يا رب!

"Accept our prayers, our Master! Accept our prayers, our Master! Accept our prayers, our Master!

Oh my Allah,

Be the air in my lungs, and be the vision in my sight.

Be the strength in my core, and be the step in my height.

Bayazeed

Spiritual Stone 11

Allah Ta'ala says in the Holy Qur'an:

وَاللَّهُ أَخْرَجَكُمْ مِنْ بُطُونِ أُمَّهَاتِكُمْ لَا تَعْلَمُونَ شَيْئًا وَجَعَلَ لَكُمُ السَّمْعَ وَالْأَبْصَارَ وَالْأَفْئِدَةَ ۙ لَعَلَّكُمْ تَشْكُرُونَ ﴿٧٨﴾

﴿النحل﴾

Translation: *"And Allah brought you out of the wombs of your mothers while you knew nothing, and He gave you hearing, sight, and hearts so perhaps you would be thankful".* (An-Nahl/78)

Oh Allah! You brought us out of the wombs and gave us life. You gave us the chance to live and to experience the sweetness of this world and the next. You gave us the chance to live and to decorate our own hereafters with eternal pleasures. You gave us the chance to live and to spread goodness. You gave us the chance to live and to end injustice. You gave us the chance to live and to help those in need. You gave us the chance to live and to witness your signs. You gave us the chance to live and to be attached with You. You gave us the chance to live and to enjoy the company of your beloved Prophet (Peace Be Upon Him) and his teachings. You gave us the chance to live and to be amongst those You love. Oh Allah, we are grateful to You, and we thank You!

Oh Allah! We came into this world while we knew nothing. We knew nothing, You gave us knowledge. We understood nothing, You gave us understanding. You taught us what we did not know. You taught us right and wrong. You taught us truth and falsehood. You taught us love and hate. You taught us happiness and sadness. You taught us success and failure. You taught us purpose and intention. You taught us divine and human. You taught us life and death. You taught us this world and the next. Oh Allah, we are grateful to You, and we thank You!

Oh Allah! You blessed us with hearing. You let us hear Your divine revelation and Your beautiful words. You let us hear the words of Your chosen one (Peace Be Upon Him). You let us hear of amazing beings like the companions (Peace Be Upon Them). You let us hear Your name and Your praise. You let us hear Your message and Your call. You let us hear Your glad tidings and warnings. You let us hear Your wants and Your pleasures. You let us hear Your messages and guidance. Oh Allah, we are grateful to You and we thank You!

Oh Allah! You blessed us with sight. You showed us the beauties of this world and its signs. You showed us the truths of this world and its deceptions. You showed us the lasting and the ending. You showed us what has gone and what is to come. You showed us what no eye can see except through Your permission. You showed us all that needed to be seen. Oh Allah, we are grateful to You and we thank You.

Oh Allah! What could we do without hearts? You blessed us with hearts. You let our hearts work. You let our hearts feel. You let our hearts taste. You let our hearts heal. You let our hearts accept. You let our hearts see. You blessed our hearts and filled it with light. You blessed our hearts and removed from them darkness. You filled our hearts with contentment and pleasure. You filled our hearts with sweetness and trust. Oh Allah, we are grateful to You and we thank You.

هَذَا مِنْ فَضْلِ رَبِّي لِيَبْلُوَنِي أَأَشْكُرُ أَمْ أَكْفُرُ وَمَنْ شَكَرَ فَإِنَّمَا يَشْكُرُ لِنَفْسِهِ وَمَنْ كَفَرَ فَإِنَّ رَبِّي غَنِيٌّ كَرِيمٌ ﴿٤٠﴾ ﴿النمل﴾

Translation: *"This is from the grace of my Lord, to test me, if I am grateful or ungrateful. And whoever is grateful, is only grateful to his own benefit. And whoever is ungrateful, then indeed my Lord is Independent and Most Generous."* (An-Naml/40)

رَبِّ أَوْزِعْنِي أَنْ أَشْكُرَ نِعْمَتَكَ الَّتِي أَنْعَمْتَ عَلَيَّ وَعَلَى وَالِدَيَّ وَأَنْ أَعْمَلَ صَالِحًا تَرْضَاهُ وَأَدْخِلْنِي بِرَحْمَتِكَ فِي عِبَادِكَ الصَّالِحِينَ ﴿١٩ النمل﴾

Translation: *"My Lord! Inspire me to always be thankful for Your favours which You have blessed me and my parents with, and to do good deeds that please You. Admit me, by Your mercy, into the company of Your righteous servants."* (An-Naml/19)

آمين يا رب! آمين يا رب! آمين يا رب!

"Accept our prayers, our Master! Accept our prayers, our Master! Accept our prayers, our Master!

Oh my Allah,

You are the centre of my galaxy,
You are the true love that I see,
You are all that is, can ever be,
You are the end in ecstasy.

Bayazeed

Praise be to Allah Ta'ala, The-True Judge and The-Real Justice. No being can judge like Allah Ta'ala, no being can understand like Allah Ta'ala, and no being can know like Allah Ta'ala. No being can be certain like Allah Ta'ala and no being can be confident like Allah Ta'ala. Allah Ta'ala is the supreme being with unfathomable understanding of every intricate detail.

Allah Ta'ala says in the Holy Qur'an:

وَنَضَعُ الْمَوَازِينَ الْقِسْطَ لِيَوْمِ الْقِيَامَةِ فَلَا تُظْلَمُ نَفْسٌ شَيْئًا ۖ وَإِنْ كَانَ مِثْقَالَ حَبَّةٍ مِنْ خَرْدَلٍ أَتَيْنَا بِهَا ۗ وَكَفَىٰ بِنَا حَاسِبِينَ ﴿٤٧ الأنبياء﴾

Translation: *"We will set up the scales of justice on the Day of Judgment, so no soul will be wronged in the least. To the extent that even a seemingly insignificant deed, a deed weighing just a mustard seed will not be ignored. Even deeds like this we shall bring out and bring to account and We are sufficient for taking account and reckoning."* (Al-Ambiyaa/47)

No person shall escape on that day, that will be the day of justice. No corrupt judgement or unfair decision will be passed that day, the judge will be none other than Allah Ta'ala Himself.

Allah Ta'ala reminds us in the Holy Qur'an:

وَإِنْ تُبْدُوا مَا فِي أَنْفُسِكُمْ أَوْ تُخْفُوهُ يُحَاسِبْكُمْ بِهِ اللَّهُ ۖ فَيَغْفِرُ لِمَنْ يَشَاءُ وَيُعَذِّبُ مَنْ يَشَاءُ ۗ وَاللَّهُ عَلَىٰ كُلِّ شَيْءٍ قَدِيرٌ ﴿٢٨٤ البقرة﴾

Translation: *"Whether you reveal what is in your hearts or conceal it, Allah will call you to account for it. He forgives whoever He wills and punishes* *whoever He wills. And Allah is Most Capable of everything.”* (Al-Baqarah/284)

Every little thing will be brought to questioning. Every oppressed person will have his chance to speak and every oppressor to ever live will be brought to justice. Those who did good shall be rewarded and fully recompensed for every good they did, and those who did wrong shall be punished for every wrong they committed.

وَوَجَدُوا مَا عَمِلُوا حَاضِرًا وَلَا يَظْلِمُ رَبُّكَ أَحَدًا ﴿٤٩ الكهف﴾

Translation: *“They will find whatever they did present directly before them. And your Lord will treat no person wrongly.”* (Al-Kahf/49)

No person's wealth will save him on that day. No person's relations will save him on that day. No person's name will save him on that day. No person's position will save him on that day. No person's intelligence will save him on that day. No person's sophisticated speech will save him on that day. That will be the day of no escape. Every man and woman, regardless of their worldly background, shall stand as equals, as slaves, before one being, before one master, The Just Creator, The All-Knowing, The All-Hearing, Allah Ta'ala.

عن عائشة رضي الله عنها أنَّ النبيَّ صلى الله عليه وسلم كان يقولُ في بعض صَلاته: "اللهمَّ حاسِبني حِسابًا يسيرًا"، فقالت عائشة: ما الحِساب اليسيرُ؟ قال: "أنْ ينظُرَ في كتابه فيتجاوَز عنه" (مسند أحمد)

Translation: *It is narrated from Aishah (May Allah Be Pleased with Her) that during some prayers The Prophet (Peace Be Upon Him) would say: “Oh Allah, Grant me an easy reckoning!”. Aishah (May Allah Be Pleased with Her) asked: “What is an easy reckoning?”. The Prophet (Peace Be Upon Him) responded: “That a person looks in his book and notices things have been overlooked and forgiven.”* (Ahmad)

Oh Allah, grant us all an easy reckoning! Oh Allah, wipe away our shortcomings and overlook our faults! Oh Allah, allow us to change our ways and allow us to turn to you before we return to you!

Oh Allah, allow us to fill our book of deeds with actions that please you! Oh Allah, You take responsibility for all those who have oppressed us, and Oh Allah, You compensate all those who we have oppressed!

Oh Allah, You blessed us with so much without us even asking You, Oh Allah, save us from the fire and bless us with paradise, and we are asking You!

آمین یا رب! آمین یا رب! آمین یا رب!

"Accept our prayers, our Master! Accept our prayers, our Master! Accept our prayers, our Master!

Oh my Allah,

How we share what shall never be shared, how we speak what shall not be spoken.

How You look where none else can see, how You fix the forever broken.

Bayazeed

Praise be to Allah Ta'ala, The-Guide. It is He who guides, and all need His guidance. Rain pours through the heavens with His guidance and wind pushes through the skies with His guidance. The one for whom Allah Ta'ala has written guidance, none can lead astray, and the one who has been left to go astray, none can guide.

The Prophet of Allah (Peace Be Upon Him) says in a Hadith:

من كان آخر كلامه لا إله إلا الله دخل الجنة (رواه أبوداود والحاكم)

Translation: *"The person whose last words proclaim, 'There is none worthy of worship besides Allah' (Laa Ilaaha Illallah)" shall enter paradise!"* (Abu Dawud & Hakim)

It is narrated from Umar Ibn Al-Khattab (May Allah Be Pleased with Him) that the Prophet (Peace be Upon Him) said:

إني لأعلم كلمة لا يقولها عبد حقاً من قلبه فيموت على ذلك إلا حرّمه الله على النار: لا إله إلاّ الله (صحيح ابن حبان)

Translation: *"Verily, I know a phrase which no servant utters truthfully from his heart and dies upon that, except the Fire is made unlawful for him. That phrase, 'Laa Ilaaha Illallah' (There is no god but Allah, there is none worthy of worship besides Allah)."* (Sahih-Ibn-Hibban)

In another Hadith it is narrated from Abu Hurairah (May Allah Be Pleased with Him) that the Prophet (Peace Be Upon Him) said:

جدّدوا إيمانكم، قيل: يا رسول الله وكيف نجدّد إيماننا؟ قال: أكثروا من قول لا إله إلاّ الله (رواه الحاكم)

Translation: *"Continue to renew and refresh your faith". It was asked: "Oh Messenger of Allah, and how should we renew and refresh our faith?". The*

Prophet (Peace Be Upon Him) responded: "Abundantly say and express that there is none worthy of worship besides Allah (Laa Ilaaha Illallah)." (Hakim)

Allah Ta'ala says in the Holy Qur'an:

$$أَمَّنْ خَلَقَ السَّمَاوَاتِ وَالْأَرْضَ وَأَنْزَلَ لَكُمْ مِنَ السَّمَاءِ مَاءً فَأَنْبَتْنَا بِهِ حَدَائِقَ ذَاتَ بَهْجَةٍ مَا كَانَ لَكُمْ أَنْ تُنْبِتُوا شَجَرَهَا ۗ أَإِلَهٌ مَعَ اللَّهِ ۚ بَلْ هُمْ قَوْمٌ يَعْدِلُونَ ﴿٦٠ النمل﴾$$

Translation: *"Is it not Allah that created the heavens and the earth for you, is it not Him that sends for you rain from the sky and then through it he brings to life beautiful gardens? You do not possess the power to bring to life even one of its trees! Can there be another god besides Allah? Absolutely not! These people who equate with Allah are people that have swerved away from justice, they have swerved away from just reasoning and equated partners with Allah".* (An-Naml/60)

Oh Allah Ta'ala, it is You that has created the skies with all its beauty, changes and complex design. If entire creation gathered together to create such a sky, they would never be able to create such a sky!

Oh Allah Ta'ala, it is You that has created this wonderful earth, with all its nature, systems and life. If entire creation gathered together to create such an earth, they would never be able to create such an earth!

Oh Allah Ta'ala, it is you that united the magnificent sky with the dazzling earth and brought forth from it beautiful gardens and fruits. If entire creation gathered together to unite the sky with the earth, they would never be able to unite the sky and the earth!

Oh Allah Ta'ala, we do not even possess the power to give life to one tree, let alone glorious gardens and the never ending forests!

Oh Allah Ta'ala, we do not even possess the power to send down one drop of rain, let alone running rivers and flowing oceans!

Oh Allah Ta'ala, it is You! You are the being worthy of worship, and there is none worthy of worship but You! You are One and you have no partner!

رَبَّنَا آمَنَّا بِمَا أَنْزَلْتَ وَاتَّبَعْنَا الرَّسُولَ فَاكْتُبْنَا مَعَ الشَّاهِدِينَ ﴿٥٣ آل عمران﴾

Translation: *"Our Lord and Master! We believe in Your revelations and we follow the messenger, so count us among those who bear witness."* (Al-Imran/53)

رَبَّنَا إِنَّنَا آمَنَّا فَاغْفِرْ لَنَا ذُنُوبَنَا وَقِنَا عَذَابَ النَّارِ ﴿١٦ آل عمران﴾

Translation: *"Our Lord and Master! We have believed, so forgive our sins and protect us from the torment of the Fire."* (Al-Imran/16)

رَبَّنَا أَفْرِغْ عَلَيْنَا صَبْرًا وَتَوَفَّنَا مُسْلِمِينَ ﴿126 الأعراف﴾

Translation: *"Our Lord and Master! Shower us with patience and perseverance, and let us die in submission to You, as Muslims."* (Al-A'araf/126)

آمين يا رب! آمين يا رب! آمين يا رب!

"Accept our prayers, our Master! Accept our prayers, our Master! Accept our prayers, our Master!

Oh my Allah,

Take me to a secret palace,
Let it just be me and You.

Squeeze me with affection,
Light, come through.

Bayazeed

Spiritual Stone 14

Allah Ta'ala says in the Holy Qur'an:

وَلَقَدْ نَصَرَكُمُ اللَّهُ بِبَدْرٍ وَأَنْتُمْ أَذِلَّةٌ فَاتَّقُوا اللَّهَ لَعَلَّكُمْ تَشْكُرُونَ ﴿١٢٣ آل عمران﴾

Translation: *"Allah helped you at the battle of Badr when you were helpless. So be mindful of Allah, perhaps you will be grateful."* (Al-Imran/123)

It was the first major battle of Islam. It was the Battle of Badr. The Muslims were few in number and the enemy were many. All odds were against them. Outnumbered and ill-equipped, the Sahabah (May Allah Be Pleased with Them) and the Prophet (Peace Be Upon Him) placed their hopes in Allah Ta'ala and advanced.

Minds were left baffled and souls were left trembling. It was a decisive victory for the Muslims and a major blow to the opposition. It was the first major step in the global spread of Islam and a turning point for the pages of history. The witnessing of events gave the Muslims massive spiritual upliftment, and the opposing world was left on shaky legs. Things were about to change.

Allah Ta'ala reminds us of the incident:

إِذْ يُغَشِّيكُمُ النُّعَاسَ أَمَنَةً مِنْهُ وَيُنَزِّلُ عَلَيْكُمْ مِنَ السَّمَاءِ مَاءً لِيُطَهِّرَكُمْ بِهِ وَيُذْهِبَ عَنْكُمْ رِجْزَ الشَّيْطَانِ وَلِيَرْبِطَ عَلَى قُلُوبِكُمْ وَيُثَبِّتَ بِهِ الْأَقْدَامَ ﴿١١/الأنفال﴾

Translation: *"Remember when He caused drowsiness to overcome you, giving you serenity, as an assurance from Him. And He sent down rain from the sky to purify you, to free you from the whispers of the devil, to strengthen your hearts, and to grant you firm feet."* (Al-Anfal/11)

Allah Ta'ala sent such a wave of peace and calm upon the believers that they were being overcome by drowsiness and sleepiness. Allah Ta'ala sent down unseen assistance to the believers and removed all their doubts. Allah Ta'ala strengthened their hearts in the face of adversity and gave them firmness.

Today, resting on luxurious beds and leaning on silky sofas, humankind is struggling to sleep. Once upon a time, men like the Sahabah (May Allah Be Pleased with Them) were walking towards the enemy and feeling sleepy. Peace is from Allah Ta'ala!

Today, surrounded by solid walls, sitting in royal and guarded apartments, humankind is in stress and worry. Once upon a time, men like the Sahabah (May Allah Be Pleased with Them) were calm and overcome by ease amid a heated battle. Comfort is from Allah Ta'ala!

Today, drowned in entertainment and play, humankind is in fear and restlessness. Once upon a time, men like the Sahabah (May Allah Be Pleased with Them) were peaceful and content realising everything they had was potentially going to be stripped away. Happiness is from Allah Ta'ala!

اللَّهُمَّ أَصْلِحْ لِي دِينِي الَّذِي هُوَ عِصْمَةُ أَمْرِي، وَأَصْلِحْ لِي دُنْيَايَ الَّتِي فِيهَا مَعَاشِي، وَأَصْلِحْ لِي آخِرَتِي الَّتِي فِيهَا مَعَادِي، وَاجْعَلِ الْحَيَاةَ زِيَادَةً لِي فِي كُلِّ خَيْرٍ، وَاجْعَلِ الْمَوْتَ رَاحَةً لِي مِنْ كُلِّ شَرٍّ (صحيح مسلم)

Translation: "Oh Allah! Set my faith straight, faith is my protection in every matter. Set my worldly life straight, in it is my livelihood and living. Set my hereafter straight, that is my place of return. Make life a means of increased goodness for me in every sense, and make death a means of peace and comfort for me from every bad and evil." (Muslim)

آمين يا رب! آمين يا رب! آمين يا رب!

"Accept our prayers, our Master! Accept our prayers, our Master! Accept our prayers, our Master!"

Oh my Allah,

Let us fall together through the heavens
endlessly, let me drop into Your arms
effortlessly.

Bayazeed

Abdullah Ibn Abbas (May Allah Be Pleased with Him) was a paternal cousin of the Prophet (Peace Be Upon Him). He was specially known for the great knowledge and wisdom he possessed. The Prophet (Peace Be Upon Him) had directly supplicated for him to be granted such knowledge and wisdom.

He spent much of his time in the blessed service and companionship of the Prophet (Peace Be Upon Him). The relationship he had with the Prophet (Peace Be Upon Him) was rather intimate and strong from an early age.

Once Abdullah Ibn Abbas (May Allah Be Pleased with Him) was sharing a riding animal with the Prophet (Peace Be Upon Him). He was sat mounted behind the Prophet (Peace Be Upon Him) when the Prophet (Peace Be Upon Him) began to address him:

يا غُلامُ إِنِّي أُعلِّمُكَ كلماتٍ، احفَظِ اللهَ يحفَظْكَ، احفَظِ اللهَ تَجِدْهُ تُجاهَكَ، إذا سألتَ فاسألِ اللهَ، وإذا استَعَنتَ فاستَعِن باللهِ، واعلَم أنَّ الأُمَّةَ لو اجتَمَعت على أن يَنفَعوكَ بشيءٍ لم يَنفَعوكَ إلَّا بشيءٍ قد كتَبَهُ اللهُ لَكَ، وإن اجتَمَعوا على أن يضرُّوكَ بشيءٍ لم يضرُّوكَ إلَّا بشيءٍ قد كتَبَهُ اللهُ عليكَ، رُفِعَتِ الأقلامُ وجفَّتِ الصُّحفُ (رواه الترمذي)

Translation: *"Young man, I shall teach you some words (of advice). Remain conscious of Allah, and Allah will take care of you. Be mindful of Allah, and you will find Him in front of you. When you ask, ask Allah. When you seek help, seek the help of Allah. And know that if the whole world were to gather to benefit you in anyway, they would only benefit you so much that Allah had already prescribed for you. And if they were to all gather to try and harm you in any way, they would only harm you so much that Allah had already destined for you. The pens have been lifted and the pages have dried."* (Tirmidhi)

Oh The friends of Allah!

What sadness do they have? What have they to fear?

The Master is with them,

Close in every moment, gentle, caring, near!

Oh The friends of Allah!

What sadness do they have? What have they to fear?

Nothing can ruin them,

Allah's pleasure, only that they hold dear!

Oh The friends of Allah!

What sadness do they have? What have they to fear?

The world can't change them,

They change the world, with just one tear!

أَلَا إِنَّ أَوْلِيَاءَ اللَّهِ لَا خَوْفٌ عَلَيْهِمْ وَلَا هُمْ يَحْزَنُونَ ﴿٦٢ يونس﴾

Translation: "*Behold! Verily the friends of Allah have nothing to fear, nor shall they be sad!*" (Yunus/62)

اللَّهُمَّ اهْدِنِي فِيمَنْ هَدَيْتَ، وَعَافِنِي فِيمَنْ عَافَيْتَ، وَتَوَلَّنِي فِيمَنْ تَوَلَّيْتَ، وَبَارِكْ لِي فِيمَا أَعْطَيْتَ، وَقِنِي شَرَّمَا قَضَيْتَ، إِنَّهُ لَا يَذِلُّ مَنْ وَالَيْتَ، تَبَارَكْتَ رَبَّنَا وَتَعَالَيْتَ (مسند احمد)

Translation: "*O Allah, guide me with those whom You have guided, and keep me in ease with those whom You have granted ease. Be my protecting friend and take me into Your care alongside others whom You have befriended and*

taken into Your care. Bless me in all that You have given me and protect me from the evil You have determined. Surely, the one in Your care shall never be humiliated, You are Blessed, You are our Lord, You are The Exalted."
(Ahmad)

آمين يا رب! آمين يا رب! آمين يا رب!

"Accept our prayers, our Master! Accept our prayers, our Master! Accept our prayers, our Master!"

Oh my Allah,

To feel Your love and affection,
Close, warm, hugged, caressed!

The wealth of all the worlds,
What else has man been blessed?

Bayazeed

Allah Ta'ala says in the Holy Qur'an:

هُوَ الْأَوَّلُ وَالْآخِرُ وَالظَّاهِرُ وَالْبَاطِنُ وَهُوَ بِكُلِّ شَيْءٍ عَلِيمٌ ﴿٣ الحديد﴾

Translation: *"He is The-First and The-Last, The-Apparent and The-Hidden, and He has knowledge of all things"* (Al-Hadid/3)

Allah Ta'ala is The-First, there is none before Him. Allah Ta'ala has been there forever, but everything else was once brought into existence.

Allah Ta'ala is The-Last, there is none after Him. Everything else has been appointed a time, the world and all creation shall be ended, but Allah Ta'ala shall remain forever.

Allah Ta'ala is The-Apparent. Sincere seekers find Allah Ta'ala wherever they go, everything that falls before their eyes leads to one Allah Ta'ala.

Allah Ta'ala is The-Hidden. Those overtaken by arrogance and desire can never see Allah Ta'ala. Even if the most divine of miracles sits before such a soul, the blind soul can never see.

Allah Ta'ala is The-All Knowing. He has complete knowledge of all that there is, was, and shall ever be.

Oh Allah! You are The-First and The-Last! From You I came and to You I shall return. Oh Allah! My beginning was only through Your pleasure, and my ending shall be with Your pleasure. Let my life and all that remains be for Your pleasure, and in Your pleasure!

Oh Allah! You are The-Apparent and The-Hidden, You open the eyes You wish to open, and the eyes You let close none can ever open! Oh Allah! Open my eyes and heart and keep them open! Show me the truth! Grant me the strength to accept the truth! Forever, keep me firmly upon the truth!

Oh Allah! You are The-All Knowing, the being with complete knowledge of all that exists! You know all from top to bottom, from start to finish! Oh Allah! Grant me such knowledge that pleases You! Save me from deceit and corruption! Cover my faults and keep me under the constant shade of Your love and mercy!

اللهم أغفر لي ذنبي كله دقه وجله وعلانيته وسره وأوله وآخره (رواه مسلم)

Translation: *"Oh Allah! Forgive my sins, all of them. Forgive the small sins and forgive the big sins! Forgive the open sins and forgive the hidden sins! Forgive the first of my sins and forgive the last of my sins!"* (Muslim)

آمين يا رب! آمين يا رب! آمين يا رب!

"Accept our prayers, our Master! Accept our prayers, our Master! Accept our prayers, our Master!"

Oh my Allah,

You are my future and
You are my past!

You are The First and You
are The Last!

Bayazeed

Allah Ta'ala says in the Holy Qur'an:

فَاذْكُرُونِي أَذْكُرْكُمْ وَاشْكُرُوا لِي وَلَا تَكْفُرُونِ ﴿١٥٢ البقرة﴾

Translation: "*Remember Me, I will remember you. And thank Me, and never be ungrateful.*" (Al-Baqarah/152)

In a lengthy Hadith the Prophet (Peace Be Upon Him) says:

إِنَّ لِلهِ تَبَارَكَ وَتَعَالَى مَلَائِكَةً سَيَّارَةً فُضُلًا، يَتَتَبَّعُونَ مَجَالِسَ الذِّكْرِ، فَإِذَا وَجَدُوا مَجْلِسًا فِيهِ ذِكْرٌ، قَعَدُوا مَعَهُمْ، وَحَفَّ بَعْضُهُمْ بَعْضًا بِأَجْنِحَتِهِمْ، حَتَّى يَمْلَأُوا مَا بَيْنَهُمْ وَبَيْنَ السَّمَاءِ الدُّنْيَا، فَإِذَا انْصَرَفُوا عَرَجُوا وَصَعِدُوا إِلَى السَّمَاءِ.

Translation: "*Allah Ta'ala has a set of special angels that roam around and search for gatherings in which Allah Ta'ala is being remembered. When they find such gatherings, they sit with them, folding their wings around one another, until they fill the entire space between them and the lowest heaven. Once the people have all departed from the gathering, the angels rise and go up to the heavens.*"

قَالَ: فَيَسْأَلُهُمُ اللهُ عَزَّ وَجَلَّ وَهُوَ أَعْلَمُ بِهِمْ: مِنْ أَيْنَ جِئْتُمْ؟ فَيَقُولُونَ: جِئْنَا مِنْ عِنْدِ عِبَادٍ لَكَ فِي الْأَرْضِ، يُسَبِّحُونَكَ وَيُكَبِّرُونَكَ وَيُهَلِّلُونَكَ وَيَحْمَدُونَكَ وَيَسْأَلُونَكَ. قَالَ: وَمَا يَسْأَلُونِي؟ قَالُوا: يَسْأَلُونَكَ جَنَّتَكَ.

Translation: "*The Prophet (Peace Be Upon Him) said, then Allah Ta'ala asks the angels although he already knows about them: Where have you come from? They respond: We have come from some servants of Yours on Earth. Servants that were glorifying You, exalting you, and claiming Your oneness. They were praising You, and they were making requests. Allah Ta'ala then asks: What are they requesting? They respond: They are asking for Your paradise.*"

قَالَ: وَهَلْ رَأَوْا جَنَّتِي؟ قَالُوا: لَا أَيْ رَبِّ، قَالَ: فَكَيْفَ لَوْ رَأَوْا جَنَّتِي! قَالُوا: وَيَسْتَجِيرُونَكَ، قَالَ: وَمِمَّ يَسْتَجِيرُونِي؟ قَالُوا: مِنْ نَارِكَ يَا رَبِّ، قَالَ: وَهَلْ رَأَوْا نَارِي؟ قَالُوا: لَا، قَالَ: فَكَيْفَ لَوْ رَأَوْا نَارِي!

Translation: *"Allah Ta'ala then says: And have they seen My Paradise? They say: No, O Lord. He says: Then how would it be if they were to have seen My Paradise! The angels then say: And they ask protection of You. He says: What do they seek My protection from? They respond: From Your Hell-fire, O Lord. He says: And have they seen My Hell-fire? They say: No. He responds: Then how would it be if they were to have seen My Hell-fire!"*

قَالُوا: وَيَسْتَغْفِرُونَكَ، قَالَ فَيَقُولُ: قَدْ غَفَرْتُ لَهُمْ، وَأَعْطَيْتُهُمْ مَا سَأَلُوا، وَأَجَرْتُهُمْ مِمَّا اسْتَجَارُوا، قَالَ يَقُولُونَ: رَبِّ فِيهِمْ فُلَانٌ، عَبْدٌ خَطَّاءٌ إِنَّمَا مَرَّ فَجَلَسَ مَعَهُمْ، قَالَ فَيَقُولُ: وَلَهُ غَفَرْتُ؛ هُمُ الْقَوْمُ، لَا يَشْقَى بِهِمْ جَلِيسُهُمْ (متفق عليه)

Translation: *"The angels then say: And they ask for Your forgiveness. The Prophet (Peace Be Upon Him) said: Then Allah Ta'ala says: I have forgiven them and I have given them what they have asked for, and I have granted them the protection they seek! The Prophet (Peace Be Upon Him) said: The angels then say: O Lord, among them is so-and-so, a much sinning servant who just happened to be passing by and sat down with them. The Prophet (Peace Be Upon Him) said: Allah Ta'ala then says: I have forgiven him too. This is such a group of people that no person who sits amongst them shall be deprived!"*
(Bukhari & Muslim)

Oh Allah! Include us in these blessed gatherings again and again! Save us from the fire! Forgive us and enter us into Your paradise!

آمين يا رب! آمين يا رب! آمين يا رب!

"Accept our prayers, our Master! Accept our prayers, our Master! Accept our prayers, our Master!"

Oh my Allah,

To have just You,
Is to have all one can need.

What are endless desires?
You are The Endless, cure my greed.

Bayazeed

Prophet Ibrahim (Peace Be Upon Him) was an exemplary character. He was a man full of wisdom, sincerity, and devotion. Again and again Allah Ta'ala mentions Him in the Qur'an. In his ways lie everlasting guidance.

Allah Ta'ala says in the Holy Qur'an:

وَمَنْ يَرْغَبُ عَنْ مِلَّةِ إِبْرَاهِيمَ إِلَّا مَنْ سَفِهَ نَفْسَهُ ۚ وَلَقَدِ اصْطَفَيْنَاهُ فِي الدُّنْيَا ۖ وَإِنَّهُ فِي الْآخِرَةِ لَمِنَ الصَّالِحِينَ ﴿١٣٠ البقرة﴾

Translation: *"And who can turn away from the way and creed of Ibrahim except a fool? We certainly chose him in this life, and in the Hereafter, he will surely be among the righteous."* (Al-Baqarah/130)

From his outstanding qualities was an unwavering faith. He was ready to be slowly burnt alive in a scorching fire, but he was not ready to denounce his faith. He was ready to turn away from the ones he loved, but he was not ready to turn away from the orders of his Lord. He was ready to put his whole world on the line at any time for Allah Ta'ala, but not for one moment was he ready to risk his friendship with Allah Ta'ala.

إِذْ قَالَ لَهُ رَبُّهُ أَسْلِمْ قَالَ أَسْلَمْتُ لِرَبِّ الْعَالَمِينَ ﴿١٣١ البقرة﴾

Translation: *"When His Lord told him to submit and surrender himself, he responded, I submit and surrender to the Lord of all the worlds"* (Al-Baqarah/131)

As a result, not only did Allah Ta'ala raise his rank in the hereafter, even in this world, Allah Ta'ala raised him to an unthinkable rank. Not only did Allah Ta'ala secure His protection in the hereafter, even in this world, Allah Ta'ala protected him in unimaginable ways.

إِنَّمَا أَمْرُهُ إِذَا أَرَادَ شَيْئًا أَنْ يَقُولَ لَهُ كُنْ فَيَكُونُ ﴿٨٢ يس﴾

Translation: *"Verily His situation is such, when He wishes something, He simply says "Be!", and it is!" (Yaseen/82)*

Be! Is all it takes, before all, it is!

Submission to One Allah, His you are, Be His!

May Allah Ta'ala bless us all with the qualities of Prophet Ibrahim (Peace Be Upon Him).

اللَّهُمَّ أَسْلَمْتُ وَجْهِي إِلَيْكَ، وَفَوَّضْتُ أَمْرِي إِلَيْكَ، وَالْجَأْتُ ظَهْرِي إِلَيْكَ رَغْبَةً وَرَهْبَةً إِلَيْكَ، لَا مَلْجَأً وَلَا مَنْجَا مِنْكَ إِلَّا إِلَيْكَ، اللَّهُمَّ آمَنْتُ بِكِتَابِكَ الَّذِي أَنْزَلْتَ، وَبِنَبِيِّكَ الَّذِي أَرْسَلْتَ (متفق عليه).

Translation: *"Oh Allah! I submit myself to you and turn to You! I hand over all my matters to You and leave my complete reliance upon You! Out of desire for You and fear for You (desire of Your love and pleasure, and fear of Your punishment and displeasure)! There is no safe haven or shelter away from You, only with You! I believe in the book You have revealed and the messenger You have sent!" (Bukhari & Muslim)*

آمين يا رب! آمين يا رب! آمين يا رب!

"Accept our prayers, our Master! Accept our prayers, our Master! Accept our prayers, our Master!

Oh my Allah,

Stand by my side,
Be with me and for me.

What else is all else?
Oh Universe, ignore me.

Bayazeed

Oh Allah! You are The-Master, and we are the servants! Oh Allah! You are The-Creator, and we are the creation! Oh Allah! You are The-Independent, and we are the dependent. Oh Allah! You are everything without us and we are nothing without You! We came from You and we have been created for You!

وَمَا خَلَقْتُ الْجِنَّ وَالْإِنْسَ إِلَّا لِيَعْبُدُونِ ﴿٥٦ الذاريات﴾

Translation: *"And I have only created Jinn and Man so that they may worship me!"* (Az-Zariyat/56)

Oh Allah! Let our lives be for You, and what life can there be without You! Oh Allah! Let us be for You! Whose are we, if not Yours?

اللهُمَّ أَنْتَ أَحَقُّ مَنْ ذُكِرَ وَأَحَقُّ مَنْ أَعْطَى، أَنْتَ الْمَلِكُ لَا شَرِيكَ لَكَ، وَالْفَرْدُ لَا تَمْلِكُ

Translation: *"Oh Allah, You are the most worthy of being remembered from all those who are remembered, and You are most rightful to give from all those who give! You are The-King, You have no partner, and You are the one that shall never perish!"*

كُلُّ شَيْءٍ هَالِكٌ إِلَّا وَجْهَكَ لَنْ تُطَاعَ إِلَّا بِإِذْنِكَ، وَلَمْ تُعْصَ إِلَّا بِعِلْمِكَ، تُطَاعُ فَتَشْكُرُ، وَتُعْصَى فَتَغْفِرُ، أَقْرَبُ وَأَدْنَى حَفِيظٍ، حُلْتَ دُونَ الثُّغُورِ، وَأَخَذْتَ بِالنَّوَاصِي، وَكَتَبْتَ الْآثَارَ، وَنَسَخْتَ الْآجَالَ

Translation: *"Everything is to end except Your blessed being! You are the closest and nearest protector! You are the curtain against evil desires, the foreheads are in Your hands! You have pre-written the destinies, and you have predetermined the times and ages!"*

الْقُلُوبُ لَكَ مُفْضِيَةٌ، وَالسِّرُّ عِنْدَكَ عَلَانِيَةٌ، وَالْحَلَالُ مَا أَحْلَلْتَ، وَالْحَرَامُ مَا حَرَّمْتَ، وَالدِّينُ مَا شَرَّعْتَ، وَالْأَمْرُ مَا قَضَيْتَ، وَالْخَلْقُ خَلْقُكَ، وَالْعَبْدُ عَبْدُكَ

Translation: *"The hearts are open for You, and for You the hidden is clear! Permitted is what You have allowed and forbidden is what you have forbade! The way of life is what You have fixed, and the decree is what You have decided! The creation is Your creation, and the servants are Your servants!"*

وَأَنْتَ اللهُ الرَّؤُوفُ الرَّحِيمُ، أَسْأَلُكَ بِنُورِ وَجْهِكَ الَّذِي أَشْرَقَتْ لَهُ السَّمَاوَاتُ وَالْأَرْضُ بِكُلِّ حَقٍّ هُوَ لَكَ وَبِحَقِّ السَّائِلِينَ عَلَيْكَ أَنْ تَقْبَلَنِي فِي هَذِهِ الْغَدَاةِ أَوْ فِي هَذِهِ الْعَشِيَّةِ، وَأَنْ تُجِيرَنِي مِنَ النَّارِ بِقُدْرَتِكَ (المعجم الكبير)

Translation: *"You are Allah, The-Kind, The-Merciful! We ask You by the light of Your divine being that has illuminated the heavens and the earth, we ask You by every right You have and by the right of those who turn to You and ask You! We ask You that You accept us in this morning or evening, and we ask You to eternally free us from the fire by Your power and might!"* (Al-Mu'jamul-Kabir)

آمين يا رب! آمين يا رب! آمين يا رب!

"Accept our prayers, our Master! Accept our prayers, our Master! Accept our prayers, our Master!

Oh my Allah,

What am I without you?
How much You still are without me!

Every moment I see you,
For how long shall I not see?

Bayazeed

Spiritual Stone 20

Allah Ta'ala says in the Holy Qur'an:

وَالْمُؤْمِنُونَ وَالْمُؤْمِنَاتُ بَعْضُهُمْ أَوْلِيَاءُ بَعْضٍ ۚ يَأْمُرُونَ بِالْمَعْرُوفِ وَيَنْهَوْنَ عَنِ الْمُنْكَرِ وَيُقِيمُونَ الصَّلَاةَ وَيُؤْتُونَ الزَّكَاةَ وَيُطِيعُونَ اللَّهَ وَرَسُولَهُ ۚ أُولَٰئِكَ سَيَرْحَمُهُمُ اللَّهُ ۗ إِنَّ اللَّهَ عَزِيزٌ حَكِيمٌ ﴿٧١ التوبة﴾

Translation: *"And the believers, men and women, are friends and protectors of one another! They enjoin what is just and forbid what is evil, they observe regular prayers, they practice regular charity, and they obey Allah and His Messenger. It is they on whom Allah will shower His mercy; surely Allah is Almighty, All-Wise."* (At-Taubah/71)

The Messenger of Allah (Peace Be Upon Him) says in a Hadith:

المسلم أخو المسلم، لا يظلمه، ولا يخذُله، ولا يكذِبه، ولا يحقِره، التقوى ها هنا – ويشير إلى صدره ثلاث مراتٍ – بحسب امرئ من الشر أن يحقر أخاه المسلم، كل المسلم على المسلم حرامٌ: دمُه ومالُه وعِرضه (رواه مسلم)

Translation: *"A Muslim is the brother of a Muslim: he does not oppress him, nor does he fail him, nor does he lie to him, nor does he hold him in contempt. Righteousness and piety is in here – The Prophet (Peace Be Upon Him) pointed to his chest three times – It is evil enough for a man to belittle his Muslim brother and think small of him. A Muslim is entirely protected and sacred for another Muslim (it is forbidden for him to intentionally cause harm to another Muslim in any sense), his blood, his property, even his honour."* (Muslim)

Oh Allah!

One we were to be, many we have become,

Lost in hatred, the hearts are numb.

91

Oh Allah!

United we stand, divided we fall,

Away from guidance, wrath we call.

Oh Allah!

Hearts have separated, far, far away,

Alone and helpless, how long can one stay?

Oh Allah!

Remove hatred amongst us, restore brotherhood,

Let there be peace, harmony, mutual love, and mutual good.

رَبَّنَا اغْفِرْ لَنَا وَلِإِخْوَانِنَا الَّذِينَ سَبَقُونَا بِالْإِيمَانِ وَلَا تَجْعَلْ فِي قُلُوبِنَا غِلًّا لِّلَّذِينَ آمَنُوا رَبَّنَا إِنَّكَ رَءُوفٌ رَّحِيمٌ ﴿١٠﴾ الحشر﴾

Translation: "Oh our Lord! Forgive our sins, forgive our brethren who preceded us in faith, and do not let our hearts entertain any unworthy thoughts or feelings against those who believe. Oh our Lord! Verily, You are Most-Kind, Merciful!" (Al-Hashr/10)

آمين يا رب! آمين يا رب! آمين يا رب!

"Accept our prayers, our Master! Accept our prayers, our Master! Accept our prayers, our Master!

Oh my Allah,

You are my planner, You are my honour,
You are my pride.

You are my comfort, You are my friend,
You are my guide.

Bayazeed

Allah Ta'ala addresses mankind in the Holy Qur'an:

$$\text{أَلْهَاكُمُ التَّكَاثُرُ، حَتَّى زُرْتُمُ الْمَقَابِرَ} \quad \text{﴿١-٢ التكاثر﴾}$$

Translation: *"Your want for more and more has destroyed you! Right till you visit your graves!"* (At-Takathur/1-2).

Oh Mankind! You are being destroyed by your own wants and worldly greed! Your obsession with power and wealth is destroying you! Your obsession with honour and pride is destroying you! Your obsession with name and fame is destroying you! Oh Mankind! What are you doing and where are you going? Do you not know of the long journey before you? Your graves are waiting and soon the realities shall be before you!

$$\text{كَلَّا سَوْفَ تَعْلَمُونَ، ثُمَّ كَلَّا سَوْفَ تَعْلَمُونَ} \quad \text{﴿٣-٤ التكاثر﴾}$$

Translation: *"But no! Whatever the case, soon you will understand! Nay, indeed! Soon you will understand!"* (At-Takathur/3-4)

Whose life had value and whose was wasted? Soon all shall know! What was worth striving for and what was useless? Soon all shall know! Whose efforts were profitable and whose were destroying? Soon all shall know!

$$\text{كَلَّا لَوْ تَعْلَمُونَ عِلْمَ الْيَقِينِ} \quad \text{﴿٥ التكاثر﴾}$$

Translation: *"If only you understood the reality!"* (At-Takathur-5)

If only you knew what was good for you! If only you knew how short-lived this life truly was! If only you knew what was actually important! If only you knew about all that still awaits!

لَتَرَوُنَّ الْجَحِيمَ ﴿٦ التكاثر﴾

Translation: *"You will certainly see the Hellfire!"* (At-Takathur/6)

The Fire you were warned of again and again will be right there before you and finally it will be too late. Punishment for every oppression and injustice! Unimaginable sorrow and sadness for every wrong and evil ever committed!

ثُمَّ لَتَرَوُنَّهَا عَيْنَ الْيَقِينِ ﴿٧ التكاثر﴾

Translation: *"Again, most certainly you will see it, you shall witness its reality with your own eyes!"* (At-Takathur/7)

ثُمَّ لَتُسْأَلُنَّ يَوْمَئِذٍ عَنِ النَّعِيمِ ﴿٨ التكاثر﴾

Translation: *"Then, on that day you shall be questioned about the blessings!"* (At-Takathur/8)

Our lives are astray dear Lord, set them straight!

You wait for us dear Lord, for what do we wait?

Moments are passing dear Lord, soon it shall be too late!

Right choices and right paths, dear Lord, write in our fate!

آمين يا رب! آمين يا رب! آمين يا رب!

"Accept our prayers, our Master! Accept our prayers, our Master! Accept our prayers, our Master!

Oh my Allah,

Lost is my heart,
It wavers and wanders.

Let us be found,
Eternal joy, infinite wonders.

Bayazeed

The Prophet (Peace Be Upon Him) is narrated to have said:

مَنْ أَحَبَّ لِقَاءَ اللهِ، أَحَبَّ اللَّهُ لِقَاءَهُ، وَمَن كَرِهَ لِقَاءَ اللهِ، كَرِهَ اللَّهُ لِقَاءَهُ (رواه مسلم)

Translation: *"Whosoever loves to meet Allah, Allah loves to meet him, and whosoever dislikes meeting Allah, Allah dislikes meeting him."* (Muslim)

In another Hadith the Prophet (Peace Be Upon Him) says:

إذا أحب الله العبد نادى جبريل أن الله يحب فلانا فأحبه فيحبه جبريل فينادي جبريل في أهل السماء إن الله يحب فلانا فأحبوه فيحبه أهل السماء ثم يوضع له القبول في أهل الأرض (رواه البخاري)

Translation: *"When Allah loves a servant, He calls the angel Jibraeel and tells him that He loves such and such a servant and so he should love him also; then Jibraeel loves that servant. Then Jibraeel announces to the dwellers of the sky that Allah loves such and such a servant and so they should love him also; then the dwellers of the sky love that servant, then acceptance is placed for that servant amongst the dwellers of the earth."* (Bukhari)

Allah Ta'ala says in the Holy Qur'an:

إِنَّ الَّذِينَ آمَنُوا وَعَمِلُوا الصَّالِحَاتِ سَيَجْعَلُ لَهُمُ الرَّحْمَٰنُ وُدًّا ﴿٩٦ مريم﴾

Translation: *"As for those who believe and do good, the Most Compassionate will certainly bless them with genuine love."* (Al-Maryam/96)

Oh Allah, fill our hearts with Your love and the love of all those who You love! Oh Allah, love us and make us from Your beloved servants! Oh Allah, fill our hearts with the passion to meet You and bless us with the chance to see You! Oh Allah, let our every meeting be a meeting of passionate lovers!

اللَّهُمَّ إِنِّي أَسْأَلُكَ حُبَّكَ، وَحُبَّ مَنْ يُحِبُّكَ، وَالعَمَل الَّذِي يُبَلِّغُنِي حُبَّكَ، اللَّهُمَّ اجْعَل حُبَّكَ أَحَبَّ إِلَيَّ مِن نَفْسِي، وَأَهْلِي، وَمِن الماءِ البارِدِ (رَوَاهُ الترمذِيُّ)

Translation: "Oh Allah, I ask for Your love, for the love of those whom You love, and for the love of all those deeds that take me to Your love! Oh Allah, make Your love more beloved to me than the love I have for myself, more beloved to me than the love I have for my family, and more beloved to me than cool, thirst-quenching water!" (Tirmidhi)

آمين يا رب! آمين يا رب! آمين يا رب!

"Accept our prayers, our Master! Accept our prayers, our Master! Accept our prayers, our Master!

Oh my Allah,

For how long shall I hide?
For how long shall I run?

Everywhere I turn,
All I see is one!

Bayazeed

Abu Hurairah (May Allah Be Pleased with Him) narrates from the Prophet (Peace Be Upon Him) that he said:

مَنْ نَفَّسَ عَنْ مُؤْمِنٍ كُرْبَةً مِنْ كُرَبِ الدُّنْيَا نَفَّسَ اللَّهُ عَنْهُ كُرْبَةً مِنْ كُرَبِ يَوْمِ الْقِيَامَةِ

Translation: *"Whoever removes a worldly grief from a believer, Allah will remove for him a grief from the griefs of the Day of Resurrection!"*

Oh Allah! Soften our hearts and allow us to love for our brothers what we love for ourselves. Oh Allah! Remove from us the grieves of this world and the next!

وَمَنْ يَسَّرَ عَلَى مُعْسِرٍ، يَسَّرَ اللَّهُ عَلَيْهِ فِي الدُّنْيَا وَالآخِرَةِ

Translation: *"Whoever alleviates the need of a needy person, Allah will alleviate his needs in this world and the Hereafter!"*

Oh Allah! Grant us understanding and bless us with the opportunity and ability to be of service to those in need. Oh Allah! We place our needs before You! Take personal responsibility of all our matters, cater for our every need and grant us ease in this world and the next!

وَمَنْ سَتَرَ مُسْلِمًا سَتَرَهُ اللهُ فِي الدُّنْيَا وَالآخِرَةِ

Translation: *Whoever shields or hides the misdeeds of a Muslim, Allah will shield him in this world and the Hereafter."*

Oh Allah! Why do we have such interest in other people's weaknesses and faults? Rotting away are our own hearts and characters, remove the sickness from our hearts and eyes! Allow us to see the good in others and save us from wasting away our precious lives in futile matters! Oh Allah! Forgive us for our shortcomings and cover our faults in this world and the next!

وَاللَّهُ فِي عَوْنِ الْعَبْدِ مَا كَانَ الْعَبْدُ فِي عَوْنِ أَخِيهِ (رواه مسلم)

Translation: *"Allah continues to help His slave so long as he continues to aid his brother."* (Muslim)

Oh Allah! We seek Your help in all our matters, and Your help is sufficient! Oh Allah! To help our brothers is to help ourselves! Allow us to continue helping others, and You continue to help us!

رَبَّنَا اغْفِرْ لَنَا وَلِإِخْوَانِنَا الَّذِينَ سَبَقُونَا بِالْإِيمَنِ وَلَا تَجْعَلْ فِي قُلُوبِنَا غِلًّا لِّلَّذِينَ ءَامَنُواْ رَبَّنَآ إِنَّكَ رَءُوفٌ رَّحِيمٌ ﴿١٠﴾ الحشر﴾

Translation: *"Our Master! Forgive us and our brothers, those who brought faith before us, and don't allow our hearts to entertain any unworthy thoughts about those who have attained faith. Our Master! Indeed You are The Most Kind, The Merciful!"* (Al-Hashr/10)

آمين يا رب! آمين يا رب! آمين يا رب!

"Accept our prayers, our Master! Accept our prayers, our Master! Accept our prayers, our Master!

Oh my Allah,

Rusting away was my heart,
Dusting away was my soul.

For long I was but pieces,
At last, we are whole.

Bayazeed

Praise be to Allah Ta'ala The-Master and The-Guide. Praise be to Allah Ta'ala The-Purpose and The-Light. Praise be to Allah Ta'ala The-Awesome and The-Kind.

Allah Ta'ala calls out every soul desiring a good life. Allah Ta'ala calls out every soul wanting to be saved from a life of misery. Allah Ta'ala alerts mankind in the Holy Qur'an:

مَنْ عَمِلَ صَالِحًا مِنْ ذَكَرٍ أَوْ أُنْثَى وَهُوَ مُؤْمِنٌ فَلَنُحْيِيَنَّهُ حَيَاةً طَيِّبَةً وَلَنَجْزِيَنَّهُمْ أَجْرَهُمْ بِأَحْسَنِ مَا كَانُوا يَعْمَلُونَ ﴿النحل ٩٧﴾

Translation: *"Whoever does good, whether male or female, and is a believer, We will surely bless them with a good life, and We will certainly reward them according to the best of their deeds!"* (An-Nahl/97)

Glad tidings for the righteous and God-fearing! Glad tidings for the doers of good! Allah Ta'ala shall bless them with good lives! Allah Ta'ala shall bless them with pure lives! Allah Ta'ala shall grant them lives of worth! Allah Ta'ala shall reward them in this world and the next!

وَمَنْ أَعْرَضَ عَنْ ذِكْرِي فَإِنَّ لَهُ مَعِيشَةً ضَنْكًا وَنَحْشُرُهُ يَوْمَ الْقِيَامَةِ أَعْمَى ﴿طه ١٢٤﴾

Translation: *"But whoever turns away from My reminder will certainly have a miserable life! And We will raise them up blind on the Day of Judgment."* (Taha/124)

Sorrow for those who turn away, the evil ones! Grief and misery for those who reject their Lord's guidance. They will live sorrowful lives! Lives filled with disappointment, anxiety, and never-ending depression.

Disaster and gloom they shall bring upon themselves. Their lives will be terrible in this world and the next!

Oh Man! You desire happiness but are not willing to accept the guidance given for your happiness! Oh Man! You hate misery but again and again you invite misery! Oh Man! What more can be said! Who can you blame but yourself?

Happiness I desire, You desire it too.

I say I believe, words, am I true?

Coolness I wish, yet I step in flame,

Misery for me, who can I blame?

وَخُلِقَ الْإِنْسَانُ ضَعِيفًا ﴿٢٨ النساء﴾

Translation: *"And humankind was created weak"* (An-Nisaa/28)

Oh Allah! Grant us the ability to correct our ways. Grant us the strength to accept Your guidance. Grant us the courage to leave misery for happiness.

آمين يا رب! آمين يا رب! آمين يا رب!

"Accept our prayers, our Master! Accept our prayers, our Master! Accept our prayers, our Master!

Oh my Allah,

Maybe it's knowledge, and maybe it's love, maybe just wild desire?

Be whatever it is, lit I am in Your passionate fire!

Bayazeed

Allah Ta'ala says in the Holy Qur'an:

اَلَمۡ يَعۡلَمُوۡا اَنَّ اللهَ هُوَ يَقۡبَلُ التَّوۡبَةَ عَنۡ عِبَادِهٖ وَيَاۡخُذُ الصَّدَقَاتِ وَاَنَّ اللهَ هُوَ التَّوَّابُ الرَّحِيۡمُ ﴿١٠٤ التوبة﴾

Translation: *"Do they not know that Allah accepts repentance from His servants and accepts their charity, and that Allah is The Accepter of Repentance, The Merciful?"* (At-Taubah/104)

میری قسمت میں بھی ایسا کوئی سجدہ کر دے،

جو میرے سارے گناہوں کا مداوا کر دے۔

ساری دنیا سے چرا کر مجھے اپنا کر دے،

میری مٹی کو خدایا سونا کر دے۔

Translation:

A prostration that compensates all my wrongs,

Master, write such a prostration in my destiny!

Take me away from the world and make me Yours,

Master, turn my resting place into a treasury!

میں تیرے چاہنے والا ہوں مگر ہے حسرت،

جن کو تو چاہتا ہے مجھ کو بھی ویسا کر دے۔

ایک نظر اپنے گناہگار پہ کر کے مولا،

اپنی رحمت کا حقدار ہمیشہ کر دے۔

Translation:

I am from those who seek You, but awful is my state,

Those who You want Master, like that, make me!

Have a gaze of mercy upon this sinful one,

Master, with a gaze, eternal grace, make me worthy!

آمین یا رب! آمین یا رب! آمین یا رب!

"Accept our prayers, our Master! Accept our prayers, our Master!
Accept our prayers, our Master!

وآخر دعوانا ان الحمد لله رب العالمين

**"And we conclude with the praise of Allah Ta'ala, The Master and
Maintainer of the universe!"**

Oh my Allah,

The silence beneath the stars and oh
the calmness above the skies!

We only ever loved truly, how truly
we loved a thousand lies!

Bayazeed

About The Author

Muhammad Bayazeed is a traditionally trained British Muslim scholar. He has travelled various parts of the world and has formal authorizations (Ijazah) in the major Islamic sciences, including a specialisation in the science of answering legal questions (Iftaa).

He studied at The College of Islamic Knowledge and Guidance, Jamiatul Ilm Wal Huda, Blackburn, UK. After spending eight years here under the guidance and mentorship of various notable scholars, he graduated with authentic certifications in Arabic, Qur'anic Recitation, Islamic Jurisprudence, Explanation and Commentary of The Qur'an and Hadith.

After graduating he set out on a journey to diversify his experience and world understanding, exploring different parts of the world. He spent time in Europe, travelling through France, Belgium, Holland, and Germany. He further spent time in Asia, travelling all across India.

After returning from India, he set his eyes on Africa and enrolled into Darul Iftaa Mahmudiyyah, Durban, South Africa. Here he received specialised training and authorization in answering legal questions under the supervision and mentorship of Mufti Ebrahim Desai (May Allah Ta'ala Have Mercy Upon Him).

Shortly after returning from South Africa, in March 2021, Muhammad Bayazeed officially published his first book, 'Covid-19 & The Butterfly', subtitled, 'The Inspiration'. The book remains widely available across the world through Amazon.

Soon after his first publication, Muhammad Bayazeed launched his own official YouTube channel, 'TheSinfulSlave'. The channel remains in its early stages and looks to gradually develop with time.

Muhammad Bayazeed is currently working on several academic and scholarly publications from his hometown in England. Besides that, he is also undertaking further studies in professional counselling.

Printed in Great Britain
by Amazon

77907889R00068